Telling

Telling

Stories of Resilience from Nairm Marr Djambana

Edited by Sina Summers

This is a Magabala Book

LEADING PUBLISHER OF ABORIGINAL AND
TORRES STRAIT ISLANDER STORYTELLERS.

CHANGING THE WORLD, ONE STORY AT A TIME.

First published 2023
Magabala Books Aboriginal Corporation
1 Bagot Street, Broome, Western Australia
Website: www.magabala.com
Email: sales@magabala.com

Magabala Books receives financial assistance from the Commonwealth Government through the Australia Council, its arts advisory body. The State of Western Australia has made an investment in this project through the Department of Local Government, Sport and Cultural Industries. Magabala Books would like to acknowledge the generous support of the Shire of Broome, Western Australia.

Magabala Books is Australia's only independent Aboriginal and Torres Strait Islander publishing house. Magabala Books acknowledges the Traditional Owners of the Country on which we live and work. We recognise the unbroken connection to traditional lands, waters and cultures. Through what we publish, we honour all our Elders, peoples and stories, past, present and future. Aboriginal and Torres Strait Islander peoples should be aware this publication may contain the images, names and words of deceased people.

Cover Design Jo Hunt
Typeset by Post Pre-press Group
Printed and bound by Griffin Press, South Australia

ISBN (Print) 978-1-925768-02-2
ISBN (ePUB) 978-1-925768-03-9
ISBN (ePDF) 978-1-925-768-04-6

A catalogue record for this book is available from the National Library of Australia

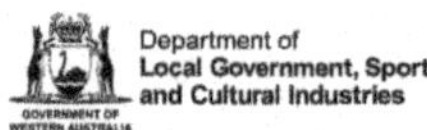

This book is dedicated to the 12 resilient members of our community who have graciously shared their extraordinary life stories, and to Aunty Roseina, who did not get to see her story in this book but whose storyline will live on.

Nairm Marr Djambana and the writers thank Sina Summers for her editing assistance.

Contents

Foreword

Nairm Marr Djambana Aboriginal Association is a place of gathering and connection for Aboriginal and Torres Strait Islander people. This collection of stories is the product of that connection, and is itself an important kind of gathering.

Thank you to the contributors with whom Nairm Marr Djambana has built a connection over so many years, who have so openly and generously given their stories and memories. Each of your highly valued life stories bring incredible insights and knowledge for us all to learn from.

Telling is important in so many ways. The lives shared on these pages are a gift to us as readers.

Deb Mellet
Nairm Marr Djambana – Gathering by the Bay

Aunty Dyan Summers

Aunty Dyan (Dy) Summers

Bunurong Traditional Owner

I am the second eldest of seven children; six girls and one boy. My parents were Maisie West and Edwin (Ted) Shaw. I'm a proud mother of six – four daughters and two sons – and I have 16 grandchildren and nine great-grandchildren.

I was born in 1952 in Launceston, Tasmania. However, it is the beautiful Flinders Island, with its snow-white sand and pristine waters, that holds my fondest memories of growing up. This is where I lived with my parents and six siblings. Our small family home was often home to our extended family too. We lived in a very close-knit community, due to my mother's Aboriginal heritage.

Flinders Island was a somewhat racist place when I was a child. Because of my father's European background, we were told that we didn't quite make the grade to identify either as Aboriginal or as white Australian. My mother always referred to herself and her family as Bass Strait Islanders. We knew that meant we had what was termed as 'black blood' although we were never allowed to speak openly about this outside of our family and extended family. If we did, we were very firmly put in our place and reminded that we weren't really Black and we weren't fully white either. We were Bass Strait Islander people.

I now know that this meant that we came from the first Bunurong people who were kidnapped and taken to Cape Barren Island in the Bass Strait by Irish sealers. My Bunurong grandmother's name was Nandergoroke, although she was given the English name Elizabeth, and she was lovingly known by her family and community as Granny Betty or Granny Maynard. She was sold to a sealer by the name of Richard Maynard, who she married and with whom she had a large family. Granny Betty was the mother of the first Bunurong family born outside of Victoria, on the Bass Strait Islands, and her children were known as the Tasmanian Bunurong or Bass Strait Bunurong people.

Granny Betty was kidnapped from her traditional land at Point Nepean on the Mornington Peninsula in south-east Victoria. Bunurong people were one of the biggest groups of Aboriginal people belonging to the Kulin Nation.

Tasmanian-born Bunurong women – Margery Munro is at the back and Mary Armstrong Maynard in the front.

Sarah Maynard

Nandergoroke was the wife of Derrimut, a highly respected chief of the Bunurong. She was heavily pregnant when George Meredith kidnapped her on 3 January 1837. Three other Aboriginal women and children were kidnapped that same day. One of the women was Doogbyerumboreoke, who was given the European name of Margery. She was kidnapped along with her two daughters Naynargorerote and Borodangergoroke as well as Granny Betty. Doogbyerumboreoke was sold to James Munro. It was James Munro who saw the economic viability of catching and processing muttonbirds. It was Doogbyerumboreoke (Margery Munro) and Nandergoroke (Granny Betty/Elizabeth Maynard) who taught Munro how to catch and process the muttonbirds as they are processed today. These four women are the ancestral grandmothers of almost all the families connected to Cape Barren and Flinders Islands.

My Granny Betty was a resilient woman. She gave birth to her children on Cape Barren Island without any medical assistance.

Granny Betty standing outside the house she lived in on Cape Barren Island. Note her clothing made of hessian sack.

Although living on a remote island a long way from her homeland was tough, the other women there supported her. I find it hard to imagine her being forced into a marriage with a man she didn't love, and then to have had a large family with him as well. She raised her children to be strong men and women, preparing them to adapt to the changes that were occurring during European settlement.

Chief Derrimut of the Bunurong people in the Kulin Nation kept looking for his beloved wife Granny Betty and his child, right up until he died. She never knew of this, although they both pined for each other. Derrimut never remarried. It is recorded in many historical research materials that he said: "No more wife, no more child, me nothing now." He died from a broken heart. It makes me sad when I think of his sorrow. I also feel very proud knowing that our Bunurong grandfather, Chief Derrimut, never stopped loving his beloved wife Nandergoroke, my Granny Betty – and she never stopped loving him. Their story is filled with both abiding love and incredible pain.

My childhood family life growing up on a remote island was filled with lots of music, singing, dancing, sport and poetry. Making our own fun was a regular practice. We lived in a small old wooden house known as Kyeema. It had a really big kitchen to provide for the many family members who stayed there. There were two long home-made wooden benches on either side of the long table where everyone gathered to eat, often up to 20 or more people at one time. Dad always sat at the end of the table and at the other end it was either my mum or her brother Uncle Mark – when he was with us he sat there and Mum sat next to Dad.

With only two bedrooms, my two youngest siblings shared with my parents and the rest of us shared the other bedroom. Five of us topped and tailed sleeping in a double bed and a single bed. My parents closed off the back verandah to make an additional room for when Uncle Mark and his wife Aunty Clare were with us. This happened quite often, as Dad worked away a lot and Mum felt it was safer for all of us having her brother living with us.

The front sitting room was saved for special occasions – in fact, I cannot remember ever sitting on the sofa in that front room. The room always looked beautiful. My mum would clean the fireplace with whitewash every weekend, putting fresh wildflowers or eucalypt and yucca leaves in a vase when visitors came to our home. She dusted and polished the sideboard daily. Mum made her own polish from resin and wild beeswax. She sometimes sat in there by herself, looking through her box of cards and photos or reading letters from her five brothers who fought in WWII. I often wonder what was going through her mind.

My mother came from a large family, consisting of 12 children all born on Cape Barren Island Reserve, Tasmania. Mum was the second youngest. My mother's family lost their house and land on Cape Barren Island when the pre-War government policies forced families to leave the Reserve and move to towns and cities to find work. Mum's five brothers went off to fight in WWII and Mum had to find work in Launceston when she was a young teenager.

Her mum, my grandmother Granny Alma, died when my mum was just 15, so she never got to meet my dad or any of us

My grandmother Alma Lily West née Brown – Nandergorokes great-grandmother.

children. A beautiful framed photo of Granny Alma hung above the fireplace. Granny Alma was Nandergoroke's great-granddaughter. Her father, known as Grandfather Bunny (Henry William Brown), was Granny Betty's first-born grandchild. He was called Bunny Brown because he had big ears. He had 23 children with three wives. My Granny Alma was his firstborn child.

In Tasmania, the Aboriginal soldiers were not given recognition for their military services or allocated land under the Returned Soldiers Settlement Act 1916. Soldiers across the state were entitled to enough land to farm and make a living, but not one Aboriginal soldier received the same as their fellow comrades.

In the early 1960s racism was rife in Tasmania, and government policies stated that Aboriginal people were not allowed to date a person of status. If they did, they would be sent to prison.

In the 1970s my father, a unionist, went to Western Australia to negotiate workers' rights. He was instrumental in setting up a political group representing the Aboriginal community in Tasmania. He met Gough Whitlam during his reign in parliament to discuss the needs of Tasmanian Aboriginal people who had no representative services to assist them, especially with housing and employment. Since then, services in Tasmania have grown to the same level as all other states and territories.

At 12 and a half years old, I moved off Flinders Island with my family. The transition from a simple life with around 200 school students to nearly 700 students at Launceston State High School was too much for me. I felt disconnected from my friends and family, and I wasn't comfortable wearing a formal uniform, which included a hat and gloves. At age 14 I got expelled from high school.

Sport and music were the most popular activities in Tasmania and these were a great opportunity to get together socially. As a young adult, I became the secretary of the Aboriginal Information Service, which offered assistance in the areas of housing, emergency funding for electricity and gas bills, and a sporting committee. This service brought the community together and created a broader support network.

In the mid 1980s I moved up to New South Wales and worked with the Aboriginal Housing Office. Then, in 1988, I attended the Bicentenary Protest in Sydney. Through this event I felt empowered to learn about my rights. I thought about my mother and grandmothers, who had become emotionally suppressed and severely impacted by forced restrictions and government policies. Because of this, I was inspired to talk to other Aboriginal families about a person's right to their ancestral identity – particularly those who were taken from their original Country and forced to live somewhere else.

Woven basket kelp bowl and shell necklace made by me. The large kelp bowl was made by Nanette Shaw and the shell necklace by Aunty B.

Through these discussions I found resistance from many Aboriginal communities, both on Bunurong Country and in Tasmania. Many stated that a person was from either one or another, but not both. Because of this, I decided to wait until these conversations could be talked about more openly. This is important to my family and me, as my ancestral storyline and dual heritage is linked to Granny Betty.

Then I began travelling to and from Victoria, and this is when I connected to my Bunurong heritage. Going to Point Nepean on the Mornington Peninsula where, traditionally, the Bunurong women gave birth to their bubups (babies), I learnt about Granny Betty's past – kidnapped and stolen by sealers, she was one of the first members of the Stolen Generations in Victoria. I was so moved by what she endured that I sat on the beach and cried. The clarity of my identity emerged, derived from a new understanding of Granny Betty's horrific experiences. It changed my life.

I am only now, as an adult, learning the art of traditional weaving, through my own research. Being part of a small group of Aboriginal women coming together to learn reminds me of my aunties mending my uncles' fishing nets. The mending was part of our cultural weaving and netting practices. This is something that was not handed down to me, although learning to do it has become very natural. I guess sitting with my aunties and watching them made me feel that I had known how to do it all along. I know it will always be a part of my family tradition.

I enjoy sharing this cultural practice with other Bunurong women. Gathering the grasses for weaving is something I enjoy, although as I am getting older now I find I must rely on others who are younger to gather for me. I also gather bull kelp to make

My late husband Ronnie Summers and I.

kelp bowls. Continuing a line of creativity within my family, I have always enjoyed cooking, poetry and song writing.

Acknowledging my Granny Betty's connection to Bunurong Country, as well as Flinders and Cape Barren Islands, is very important to me, and her story is embedded into my family history. Her endurance and strength are acknowledged with pride and honour, not just by myself but also by future generations.

I proudly identify as a Bunurong Tyralore woman (children and women connected to sealers in Bass Strait), and I live between Flinders Island and the Mornington Peninsula on Bunurong Country. My dual heritage is what makes me who I am today. I'd like to see Aboriginal people tell their stories to students in schools, highlighting culture and place, and honouring the people who have lived through historic times.

Aunty Patsy Smith

Aunty Patsy Smith

Taungurung Traditional Owner

I was born in 1955 at the Mooroopna Hospital by the banks of the Goulburn River. I'm a Taungurung Traditional Owner. My great-grandparents came to Coranderrk Aboriginal Station along with many others who had been driven from their land during the years of white settlement. Known as the Coranderrk Mission, it consisted of 2,000 hectares of fertile mountain country around Healesville in Victoria's Yarra Valley. It was founded in 1863.

As a result of the Aborigines Protection Act 1886, around 60 residents were ejected from Coranderrk at the beginning of the 1890s depression. In 1893, the government reclaimed almost half of the land, and by 1924, orders came for the Station's closure.

My family was shifted north to the Cummeragunja Mission, by the Murray River on the New South Wales border. Life on the mission was hard and the managers were really cruel. The strict rules and regulations imposed on the Aboriginal community there made it impossible to survive. No one was allowed to leave without permission, there was minimal food and clothing, and extremely

My great-grandparents, Willy and Annie Hamilton, and family.

poor housing. My great-grandfather was banned from the Mission, because he would often leave to go and find food for his children, my great-grandmother and her thirteen brothers and sisters. He would then have to sneak inside at night to visit his wife and their children.

By early 1939, there had been a number of deaths at the Mission, which were attributed to the minimal rations, lack of sanitation and cramped living conditions that residents at Cummeragunja were being subjected to. This caused a majority of residents to leave in protest over the appalling conditions. This event became known as the Cummeragunja Walk-Off. My great-grandfather was involved in this.

My family moved to the flats in Shepparton, Victoria, and lived near the tip. At that time, there were about 300 people living on the river flats. My mother, Melva Roberts (née Walsh), and her sisters were fairly well known around the Shepparton area, as were my grandparents Granny Effie and Poppa Joe Walsh.

They were able to find enough materials dumped at the tip to build their own humpies. For them what was most important was to be close to their family and friends and to be able to come and go as they pleased. They earned their living by fruit picking at local fruit orchards. These were hard times and many families relied on hunting and fishing to feed their growing families.

Later on, my mother lived with my grandmother Granny Effie and Aunty Vera on the river bank with my elder siblings, Larry and Joylene. My parents were together for some years, but then my father left when I was only 12 months old. This was

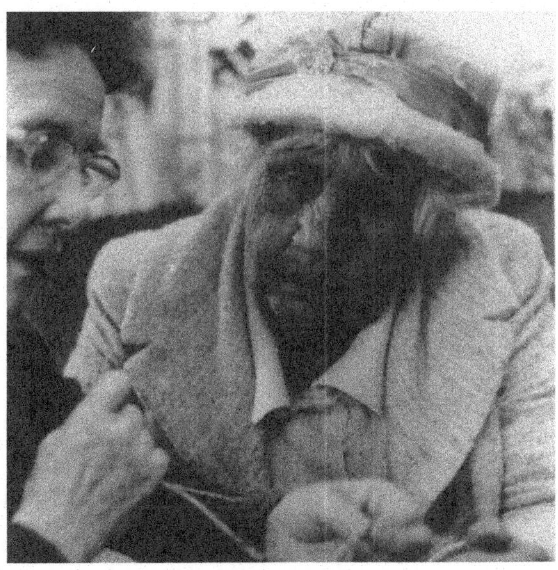

My mum.

the year of the 1956 Murray River flood, which affected all the people living on the riverbank area. Because of this catastrophic event, we moved to a different location. Within three months, the police took the three of us children, because we had no fixed abode, means of care or support. There were six children taken that day from the river flats. We appeared at the courts in Melbourne and were immediately placed under the care of the Children's Welfare Department.

At first, we were placed in Turana Reception Centre, a home for boys and girls in Parkville, Royal Park. This facility held a weekly average of 204 children at the time and was directly managed by the Victorian Government. Then, once we got permanent placements, we were moved again. My brother Larry was three years old and my sister Joylene was four. They were sent to Geelong, to the Kardinia Children's Home, run by The Salvation Army. Because I was only 12 months old, I was placed in Presbyterian Babies' Home in Camberwell, Melbourne. We were separated that day, and we didn't meet again until we were young adults.

I stayed in the Presbyterian Babies' Home for about four years, which was a bit longer than usual, due to having two hip operations. Then I went to the William Booth Memorial Home for Girls in Camberwell. The home had the capacity for about 55 girls in the 1950s, from the ages of four to 14 years old. Many of the girls were wards of the state.

My foster aunt, who was training to be a mothercraft nurse, took an interest in me and wanted to bring me into her family. Her older sister fostered me. She was a young woman who lived with her parents in St Kilda at the time, and she was told that she had to have her own home before she could take me in.

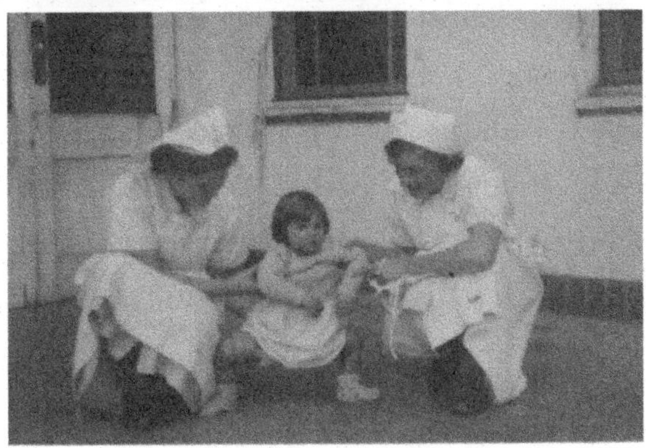

Top: Me at the orphanage wearing a leg brace.
Bottom: Me with two nurses.

Once my foster parents built their own home in Seaford, they were able to foster me. I treasure all my fond memories of growing up there. I've lived on the Mornington Peninsula ever since.

One of the starkest memories I have of living at the William Booth Memorial Home for Girls was ignited when I watched the program *Stolen* (2000). I didn't realise how strong some of my memories were. It took my breath away. I remember the beds lined up neatly, and the little brown leather suitcases that were given to all the kids there. When I left the children's home, I was given one. There was a playground there, so we had times when we were allowed to play. However, life was very structured at the home – you ate at a set time, played at a set time and you weren't allowed to talk at the table.

I remember vividly a time when I asked someone at the dining table if they could pass me the salt, and got called up immediately to the front, where The Salvation Army captains and staff were sitting. I got given the strap in front of everyone. There was no explanation.

Another time, when we were eating corned beef one evening for dinner, instead of serving the usual white sauce with it they gave us pickles. I couldn't eat it, the flavour made me feel ill. So, the staff picked up my plate and made me sit at the front, with a couple of other kids who hadn't eaten their meals, and they force fed that food into us. I think they wanted us to be grateful for our food, when other children in the world were starving. I couldn't eat pickles again until I was in my late 20s – that traumatic incident stayed with me for some time.

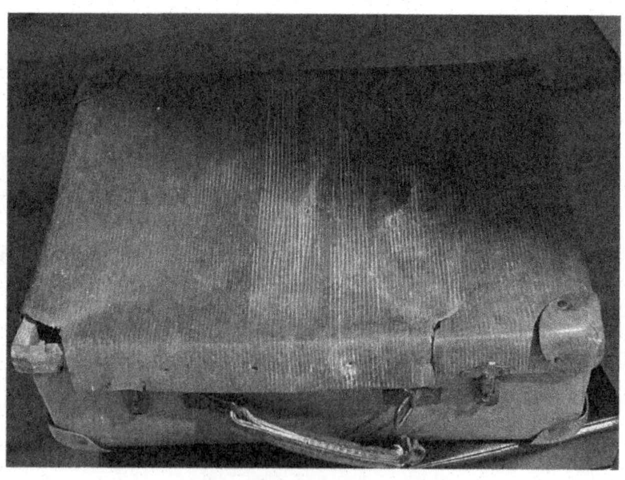

My suitcase at the orphanage.

Me at 16 years old with my foster brothers (from left) Jamie, Anthony and Paul.

I had been pestering my foster mum to take me back to the children's home, so that first year with my new family, Mum took me and my baby brother for a visit. When we arrived, I felt proud that I didn't have to stay there anymore. The Salvation Army captains greeted us at the front door and all the girls were in the lounge calling out to me. I just grabbed my younger foster brother's hand and marched out the back door, outside to the swings and slides. I felt liberated that I had the freedom to go wherever I wanted to.

While I was there, I passed a room that looked like a board-room. The door was open and on a large table were lots of Christmas presents. I could see beautiful dolls, toys and sparkly wrapping paper. It was an odd thing to see. I don't remember ever getting any gifts or celebrating Christmas while I was at the children's home. My foster mum told me that she had sent me a bride doll one year for Christmas. I never received it.

My happiest Christmas was when it was close to the time when I was allowed to live with my foster mum at Seaford and we had our first Christmas together. I woke up and there was a pram beside my bed, and it was full of toys. I was so excited that I felt overwhelmed. It was almost too much for me to bear – I couldn't even speak, so Mum helped me open the presents. The pram was navy blue, with silver sparkles that shone in the sunlight.

When I was six years old, I moved to Seaford and became part of a family, and I gained three younger brothers: James, Anthony and Paul.

I was eighteen when my older brother, Larry, came to visit me. This was when child welfare ceased guardianship of us. It was so wonderful to actually see him in person. I used to imagine what it would be like when we finally connected again. I learnt so much about my family, my history and about myself.

When I first found out about my Aboriginal heritage from my brother, Larry, I asked my foster mum why she didn't tell me that I was Aboriginal. She explained that, because of past circumstances, she thought that I might be ashamed of being of Aboriginal blood. I think she thought this was for my own protection. Larry kept in touch from time to time, however I didn't find any further information out about my family lines.

So, it wasn't until I was married and having my second child that I went to see my natural mum. My respect and love for my foster mum drove in me a loyalty to her, which led to my not contacting my natural mum. I feared losing my foster mum if I contacted my natural mum, which was ultimately what happened. Having children in my 30s, especially my daughter who had the same medical problems as me during my time in the children's

My brother Larry and I finally reunited.

home, was a very turbulent time for me. My need to activate long repressed feelings was the catalyst for connecting with my mum. Knowing she no longer had a relationship with my brother or sister at this time and that I could be rejected as well did not stop me from wanting to try to reach out. I was in my mid-30s and ready to listen and learn. We talked about many things and this inspired me to pursue a long-held desire to explore my Aboriginal identity. We were able to connect, but her health was slowly declining with dementia and our relationship eventually went the way that my brother and sister's relationships with her had gone.

I got my freedom of information records and spoke to many people in my quest to get more knowledge. It is really important to me to know my family history and to understand who I am. This is what I have passed on to my own children. It's vital that our stories are shared. Truth telling is essential for young Aboriginal people, to learn how we survived and how our resilience enabled us to achieve more than we ever imagined.

Aunty Yvonne Luke

Aunty Yvonne Luke

I'm the second eldest of five children, and I was born in 1949. I've lived in Melbourne all my life. My father fought in WWII, and when the war finished he got a loan through the War Service Homes Scheme and purchased a house in Clayton. Across the road from our house there was a big paddock and lots of trees – we used to call it the woods. I played there often with the other kids from our neighbourhood. I was a bit of a tomboy, so I enjoyed mucking about with the boys.

Because both my parents were devout Catholics. We went to Catholic school and the first one, which was the closest to where we lived, was in Oakleigh, Melbourne. My sister and I had to catch a bus every day. I was aged five and my sister was 18 months older. There were about 30 kids in each class.

Then, when I was about seven, my father purchased a block of land in Moorabbin to build our own house. My sister and I with our younger brother had to walk nearly three kilometres to our new school while we waited for our home to be built. After living there for about three years, it became obvious that there were a lot of faults with the house, so my father decided to take the building company to court. He won the case but lost all his money in the process.

Because of this, we had to move to the north side of the city to a housing commission house in Fawkner. My parents ended up buying the house. After WWII ended most Australian mothers were homemakers and didn't work. However, in the late 1960s my mum got a job up at the local bakery and she loved it, because she earned her own money and she felt independent. She also got to meet many of the other women from around the neighbourhood. After returning home after the war my father worked at the Paymaster General's Office (PMG), and then for the rest of his working life at the Melbourne Museum.

My mother, Eileen Kennedy, was born in Alyawarr Country. She was born in the Northern Territory in the early 1920s under

My mother Eileen Parsons née Kennedy, father Alfred Parsons, husband Robert Luke and me, 1982.

the rule of the Aboriginal Protectorate. Her mother, Flora, was an Aboriginal woman born in Jingili Country. Police records state that Flora died an accidental death at Elkedra Station. However, the Aboriginal people of that place tell a different story – that Flora was murdered. My mother was about four years old and was placed into St Vincent de Paul Orphanage all the way down in Adelaide, South Australia, in the suburb of Goodwood. The Catholic Church opened it in 1866 and it was run by the Sisters of Mercy. It closed in 1975 under a cloud of abuse. During her time at the orphanage, she couldn't see any of her mob. She had an older brother who she also didn't see at all. He was sent to the Christian Brothers College in Adelaide, because it was considered more important for a boy to receive an education.

My grandfather was a part-owner of Elkedra Station and lived there with his wife Monica and their four children, until he became ill in early 1939. He moved to South Australia, where he received medical treatment until his death in July 1939. His wife, Monica, was pregnant with their fifth child at this time, so she moved back to Melbourne with her children to stay with her sister.

When my mother turned 14, my grandfather and Monica got permission from the Chief Protector of Aborigines to get her released, on 9 February 1937. The letter read: "Daughter of M. F. Kennedy, Eileen, from Elkedra Station, 14 years of age, has been receiving education in Adelaide for the past ten years."

In the Northern Territory, all Aboriginal people were put under the jurisdiction of the Protector of Aborigines between 1864 and 1939. This meant that if they wanted to move anywhere, they had to get permission. In some cases, they were exempted from this system and were given the right to vote and be recognised as an

Top to bottom: The old Elkedra Cattle Station; the homestead; the jail; the Elkedra River, which runs near the homestead.

Australian citizen. When my mum's freedom came through, she was able to move in with Monica Kennedy, who had just given birth to her fifth child. She took Mum in so that she could look after her children while she worked as a nurse.

Monica received some money from the sale of the cattle station and bought a house in Malvern, Melbourne. When Monica died, around 1973, her property was divided up between her five children, with a small amount also given to my mum. Monica's children were lovely people. I spoke to Teresa, the eldest daughter, and she told me that they never knew that my mum, Eileen, was their sister. They were never told. She said: "We loved her like a sister."

My mum never talked about her past; in fact, she told us that she went to a boarding school rather than telling us it was an orphanage. She died at age 62, after being ill for many years with kidney problems. My father retired at age 55 and nursed her through this time while she was on dialysis.

My parents met a year after the war finished and got married in 1946. Mum was 23 and Dad was 27. During the war all women had to go out into the workforce and find a job. Mum worked as a telephonist at the PMG, and she earned a decent wage. She was a devout Catholic and used to go to church before she started work. My father was a strong Catholic too and went to St Francis' Church in Melbourne. Dad really loved my mum and would often visit her grave after attending mass on a Sunday.

I recall the times when our school parent-teacher nights came up and Mum never wanted to go, so Dad would go instead. She never went to anything to do with our school. Most times Mum went anywhere was when she went out with Dad. I think this was because there was racism, which caused her to feel fearful. We didn't understand this at the time, because our parents never talked about it. Mum's closest friends were from the orphanage. One particular friend, who we called Aunty Kath, used to visit Mum three or four times a year. She was put into the orphanage because her father was German. Separations and segregations occurred for a variety of reasons back then.

I learnt a bit of Mum's past from Aunty Kath. She was the one who told me that Mum grew up in an orphanage and not a boarding school.

My two sisters and I then decided to do some research about our family history. My older sister, Lorraine, was working up at Alice Springs Hospital as the Director of Social Work and Allied Health. While she was there, she met Eddie Tranter who told her, "You've got to meet your people." Both my sisters and I went

My sister, Denise Mackay, on the road to Elkedra.

Top: Alyawarr Elder Jemima, and her son.
Bottom: Me, Jemima and Denise.

exploring the area where our mum was born and Eddie came with us to introduce us to our mob.

It was amazing to be there but also very sad. The suspicions we'd had about our grandmother's murder were confirmed. It was heartbreaking to hear of her tragic death. We also met Jemima, who was about eight years old when my grandmother was murdered. She looked after Mum who was a little girl of about four years old. All the Elders we met remembered Mum and could recall the time they spent with her. It was so wonderful to hear their stories and to be welcomed in by them. They advised us of

Meeting the mob at Murray Downs Station.

our grandmother's and mother's Skin-names and also give us our Skin-names. They told us that they had been waiting a long time to meet us and asked why didn't we come earlier.

None of them knew where she had gone. Information was not shared, and no one talked about the past. Hearing about our family history was a shock and in stark contrast to what we knew about our mum. We thought she'd had a privileged upbringing and was educated at boarding school. This was the first time we heard the truth about what happened to her and to our grandmother.

I visited the orphanage in Goodwood, South Australia where Mum had lived until she was 14 years old. Aunty Kath told us that Mum never got into trouble there because she was always a good girl. She was probably so scared all the time that she didn't dare to do anything wrong. Aunty Kath went back to the orphanage to get her personal records. My sister applied for our mother's files, but there was very little information there.

In 1993, I decided to embark on a course of learning and gained an Associate Diploma in Social Science, majoring in Aboriginal Studies. This helped me in my search to find out more about my family history. I met people and went to places that connected me to my family heritage. In 1994 I went on a fact-finding tour of the Northern Territory. We were eight students and we hired two four-wheel drive vehicles. During this time, I found out a bit about my mother's brother Dan and met his daughter Eunice. We never knew much about him. Eunice was one month younger than me and was a nurse who lived in Alice Springs.

I felt really sad for my mum and wished I'd known more about her and the devastating circumstances that she'd endured. My grandmother's life was cut short in a horrific way. Mum was trying to protect us by not talking about her past.

I can remember when we were allowed to vote. I was about 18 years old and talked about this a lot with my friends. My mum was given her freedom when she left the orphanage, but a lot of Aboriginal people were not given the right to be a citizen until it was made official in 1967. After that we were able to vote. I joined the swarms of people on reconciliation marches and NAIDOC protests. There was significant inequality in wages too. I can remember when females earned 75% less than males across all sectors of the workforce.

As a young adult, I had a boyfriend who was called up for national service. We were in the same grade in primary school. When I discovered I was pregnant our relationship ended. In 1972 I gave birth to my eldest child. I was 23 years old. In 1972 single women were not eligible for a pension. My boss at work, where I had been employed since I was 15 years old told me that he would save my job until I was ready to return to work. I had hoped that my mum would be able to help me look after my son. However, she had become very ill. When my son was six months old I put him into a crèche, only to then discover that this cost me half of my wages.

In 1975, I decided to forge ahead on my own and I bought a block of land. At that time, women were not allowed to get a financial loan. However, I applied for a building society loan, which were offered to people on lower incomes. I would check the newspaper every day for the advertisement stating that you could apply, but by the following day the quota for loan applications had already been reached. There were so many people trying to borrow money that the competition was fierce. So, I wrote to a member of parliament about this problem, stating that it wasn't a fair process for people trying to get ahead in life.

My son Brenton standing in front of our new house, 1979.

I got an interview with the building society directly afterwards and received a loan for $25,000. I found a builder but he then went bankrupt. Then, after finding another builder, I finally moved into my own house with my son in 1979. It felt fantastic to be in my own home.

In 1981, I met my husband, Robert. We got married the following year and we had two daughters. Robert was originally a geologist. However, he developed skin cancer from continually working outside. After he recovered, he got a job at Australia Post and worked there for many years. When I first started work as a junior clerk, at age 15, I was doing all the wages, debtors, creditors, and sales tax, as well as all general office duties. I just learnt as I went along, without any formal training. I ended up being the company accountant. Later, I went to TAFE and then on to university. After two years of studying, I dropped out. I found it hard juggling work and after-school activities for my children. Then I got a job as a bookkeeper so that I could take my kids to sports and after school activities. It was my Associate Diploma that I really enjoyed. I was one of only three who completed it and qualified. After completing it, I took a full-time job as a Koori educator at a secondary college.

Then, I worked for the Victorian Aboriginal Community Services Association Ltd (VACSAL) at the Bert Williams Aboriginal Youth Services. When the Howard government came into power, they cut funding for youth services. Unfortunately, we at Bert Williams Aboriginal Youth Services lost our jobs. Shortly after, VACSAL employed me to work in youth justice. This work was rewarding. I helped the Koori kids through their court proceedings and visited the custodial centres. I worked there for about eight years, until I was asked to be involved with the implementation of the second phase of the Aboriginal Justice Agreement in 2006. We implemented the Children's Koori Court. We also introduced warnings and cautioning programs and developed a way to explain things to youth. We established a bail support program, a pre-and post-release program, and included a whole-family approach to supporting at risk youth, along with an increased number of youth justice workers. I worked with a working group to establish the Children's Koori Court in both Melbourne and Mildura. We went to parliament to hear the second reading of the bill to change the Children, Youth and Families Act 2005 to include the Children's Koori Court, and every political party voted for it. Now, looking back, it is disappointing that our young Aboriginal people are still overrepresented in the justice system.

I was invited to sit at the Broadmeadows Koori Court as a respected Elder. I really felt I belonged in the Victorian Aboriginal community when working in the Koori Court. I became a member of the Youth Parole Board of Victoria in 2010, and eventually retired from this position in 2019. Since 2013, I have been a board member and then a director with Baluk Arts in Mornington.

I would like to see families supported to ensure that young Aboriginal people have the opportunity to get the best education they can. In addition to this, I'd like to see diversions used more often within the justice system, so that young people can avoid the life-long effects of a criminal conviction. I think an approach where learning is promoted and families supported would lead to new pathways, building a more sustainable crime prevention system.

Uncle Mik Edwards

Uncle Mik (Erik) Edwards

I was born in 1956, the year the Olympic Games were held in Melbourne. My parents are Nugget and Mary Edwards, and I come from Balranald in New South Wales, approximately 150kms from Lake Mungo. It's old blood Country with a vast landscape. This semi-desert area and the Mallee have unique places of beauty, such as the dark grey and orange sands near the Murrumbidgee River. My nanny (Dad's mum) was also from there. Mum was a Yorta Yorta woman from the Shepparton and Goulburn Valley area.

We camped on our traditional land in one building, which had little rooms surrounding the middle area where we sat around a big open fireplace and kitchen area. Mother Nature was our place for playing, hunting, exploring and learning. Dad was a big man standing 6 foot 7, with 3 inch-wide wrists. He worked for many of the outer stations and was an excellent horseman. Later on, he used to break in some of the horses owned by Bart Cummings. Mum was a tall woman too. She worked as a local

Left: My brothers Reg (deceased), David, Wally and Kutcha.
Right: My mum Mary Edwards (deceased), me and my sisters, Maria and Alice.

picker, and Nanny would look after us kids. I am the second eldest of 12 children in my family.

I was forcibly removed from my family in 1967, along with five of my younger siblings. I was 11 years old. My life changed forever from that day. I was taken from my traditions, people, culture, spirit world, song lines, fires and lore.

I was called up on the PA system one day at primary school, while I was out on the field playing footy. The loudspeaker bellowed out the words: "Can all the Edwards children please come to the office." When I arrived, I saw my siblings Reg, Alice, Wally and Marie standing in the office, surrounded by five policemen – one per child. A welfare worker stood solemnly staring at us, and the school principal sat there in silence. No one spoke up for us or showed any concern for our safety. They told us that they were going to get our mum from the pickers' quarters and our baby brother Kutcha, who was only 12 months old. Dad was out working.

They put us into a police car and took us to where Mum was. We were all frightened beyond belief, as they kept us in the car while they took Kutcha off Mum. She was screaming, crying, desperately trying to stop them. I will never forget seeing Mum left all by herself as they drove us away, with no support, howling her eyes out. They took us in their police car to the Swan Hill Magistrates' Court, as there was no such thing as a children's court back then. As we came out of the courtroom, Mum handed Kutcha to me and told me, "Don't let him go, son." I held on to him right up until we arrived at Parkville, Victoria, at the Turana Reception Centre, a boys' home. The police tried to drag Kutcha off me but I resisted, holding on to him tightly. Eventually they ripped him from my arms and then placed him in Allambie Reception Centre, an orphanage, with my four other younger siblings.

As I was older than they were, I was sent to Turana, and the first night there was horrific. I had no shoes and was wearing a light shirt and shorts, completely unprepared for what I saw as being trapped in a children's jail. I was heartbroken and in shock – traumatised by this horrendous abduction.

Turana, once called Royal Park Depot, was the sole reception centre for children committed to state care from 1880 to 1961. The buildings were renamed in 1952, and from around 1960 the government established new reception areas, as they called them, to alleviate overcrowding at Turana. By the 1990s, the state had contracted the facility out to non-government agencies. Turana operated as a youth training centre from around 1985. The Parkville Youth Residential Centre opened on the site in 1991, and the Melbourne Youth Justice Centre opened there in 1993.

It consisted of four sections: Billabong, Poplar Cottage, Quamby House and Waratah House.

I was put into the Billabong quarters at first, although I was continually moved around all the sections. I remember my first experience there vividly. There were two bunks in the tiny room I was put in, and one other guy was already sleeping in there. He was older, and a much bigger guy than I was. I felt vulnerable and without any protection. Not long after I was shoved into the room with him, he got up from his bed and came over to me with a dark, threatening look in his eyes. I noticed his boots on the ground near his bed, so I grabbed them with lightning speed to use for my protection as he attacked me. I was charged for my attempt at defending myself, even though I was only 11 years old.

I was separated from other Aboriginal children so that we couldn't speak our language or talk about our culture. There was a lot of abuse there, and little acknowledgement of this from staff members until many years later, when a Royal Commission was instigated. The findings from this state that in some cases children admitted as wards of the department were placed with juvenile offenders. Other findings included an absence of security checks to ensure staff members were qualified, experienced and equipped to care for children. In addition to this, many of the staff were not trained to recognise sexual abuse of residents or respond effectively to their complaints. Complaints from the children were not reported, leaving the children unsafe and at risk of abuse.

The English women who worked at the cottages, however, were genuine carers and they were good to us. I had to fight to survive but they showed a lot of kindness, which I hold in appreciation.

Me, my older brother and his son, Arthur Bradley.

Me and my daughter, Teresa.

Altogether, I went to eight different institutions throughout the seven years I was kept in state care. I didn't see my siblings until I was 14. I was lonely during the three years I waited to reunite with them. I really missed them.

I went to Wattle Park Primary School and Kingswood College. Various kinds of sports were my absolute joy. I learnt the essence of teamwork and of sportsmanship. I played footy for Hawthorn at the weekends and loved it. I was a fast runner, a skill my dad pointed out to me when I was a young boy. I left the orphanage at age 18. During the mid to late 1970s, I finally re-connected with my siblings. It was an emotional reunion that we all cherished greatly.

The last day I remember being free and a totally happy human being was when I was sitting on the verandah with my mum, my aunties and my nanas before I was abducted. Although I am a happy man now, there is always a missing link in my circle of life.

I got married in my mid-20s and I am a proud father of seven children. For many years I have worked as a cultural advisor, and in conservation and land management at the Royal Melbourne Institute of Technology (RMIT). As a mentor, I work closely with people to instill cultural heritage interpretations – scar trees, medicinal plants, rock etchings and land sites. We have some of the oldest petroglyphs in the world. Mother Nature is the boss – if we look after her, we all benefit.

My message is: stay strong. When no one is there to comfort you, you must push your fears aside and rely on your inner self. There is a great sense of pride that lives within you.

Aunty Marion Hansen

Aunty Marion Hansen

(Née Green)

My mother Connie Green (née Cutmore) is a Kamilaroi woman born at Moree, in New South Wales. She was forcibly removed from her family at the young age of 12 and placed onto a farm as a domestic. The station owners would bring her into Moree now and then to visit her family. They could see that she was intelligent, so they offered her correspondence education. However, she was never given the opportunity to speak her own language.

As a young educated adult, my mother worked as a nurse's aide at the McMaster Ward, which was the Aboriginal ward, an area at the back of the Moree District Hospital. Patients would have to wait around the back until the doctors had finished their rounds before being treated.

My father was a Bundjalung man from the north coast, and he spoke his language. Unfortunately, I never learnt it. He received an education while working as a tracker for many years with the New South Wales police.

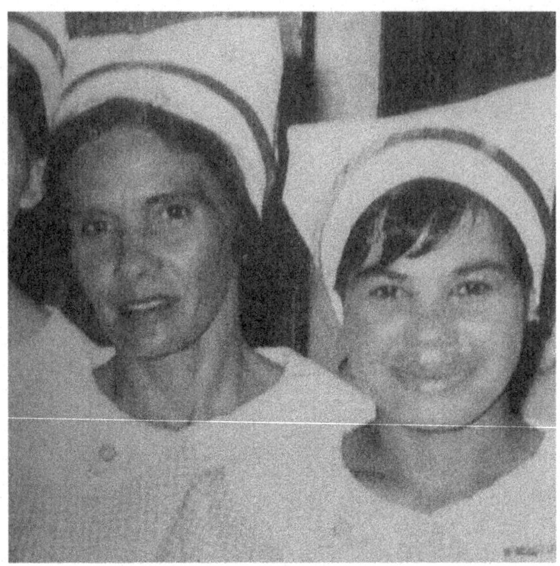

My mum Connie Green (left), nursing in Moree.

I am a Kamilaroi woman and was born in 1950 during a flood, on the new mission at Moree. I'm particularly proud that my birth certificate states that I was born on the mission and on my Country. My aunt delivered me on the mission, and then I went to the Aboriginal ward at the hospital in Moree.

My parents, my elder brother and I stayed with my aunt for a couple of years on the new mission in Moree. Then we moved to the township of Glen Innes, on the Northern Tablelands of New South Wales, where my two younger brothers were born. We lived there for many years, until the police force no longer required the services of my father, then we all moved back to the mission in Moree.

Moree was heavily policed. I remember vividly the times when we would be on the mission and someone would see dust appear as a car was coming toward us, down the long dirt road. Everyone would shout, "Jungas!" meaning police. The children would run away as fast as they could because the police would scoop up the children they caught, sometimes up to a dozen at one time, and then take them away. A lot of little kids were taken from there and you'd never see them again. One of my close friends was stolen from the mission one day, when I was about five or six years old. The police never told anyone why the kids were taken.

There was a manager at the mission, and one little school, which was packed full every week with about 30 to 40 children in the one classroom. The only teacher at the school was an elderly white woman, who insisted that the children call her Miss Sharp.

My parents always wanted a better life than they had experienced, living in little tin huts with dirt floors out in the bush at Moree. So, we moved again to Bellata, a small town in north-central New South Wales, about 35kms south of Moree. My father got a job there on the railways as a fettler. My two sisters were born there, and our family of eight lived in railway tents for nearly 10 years. The living area consisted of three main tents – one was set up as a kitchen, the second was where our parents slept, and all of us six kids slept in the third tent. We were the only Aboriginal family living in Bellata at that time.

I used to catch a train from Bellata and then a bus to the mission at Moree. I'd go to the swimming pool there and catch up with family members. Back then you had to get permission for just about everything from the mission manager. He wanted to know why you were going there, and who you were going to see. There was always a specific time that you had to leave the pool. This was all because of the government policies that were enforced in the 1960s. Living on the mission meant that families received rations of tea, sugar and flour.

Mum insisted that us children went to church and Sunday school as part of our weekly routine, and everyone helped out with family life. I bred Angora rabbits and my brother kept an aviary of birds. My fondest memories include the many occasions when all the children from around the area would get together to play cricket or rounders on the flats in front of our tents. We played all day and we would go swimming often. These were some of the best times of my life.

There was an old drover who used to go through the town, and if he had a lamb that had lost its mother, he'd give it to me to look after. I ended up with quite a few lambs, and then as they got older the drover would take them back again. There was one lamb, however, who I named Buster – he grew into a woolly, curly-horned ram who used to run around with the kids out on the field when we played cricket. He followed me everywhere, although he'd get so hot racing up and down with all the children that he often fainted with exhaustion. I'd have to hose him down with water to cool him off and bring him around again.

I went to high school at Narrabri, 42kms south of Bellata, because my parents wanted me to complete my education without the constant influence of racism, which was rife in Moree. My enthusiasm for learning was rewarded with a bursary, which gave me an opportunity to go to a ladies' college.

Unfortunately, I didn't get there due to family issues. When I was about 15 years old, we moved back to Moree and I got a job as a telephonist at the Moree Post Office. I worked there until my early 20s. My cousin and I were the only two Aboriginal employees working there at the time.

The high Aboriginal population living in Moree was subjected to harsh restrictions. The segregation in Moree was like apartheid. It was really bad. There were thousands of Aboriginal people living in Moree, some residing on the two missions there and others in small huts in the bush. We were not allowed to go to the public pool or the indoor movie theatre, and if you wanted to go to the outdoor movie theatre you had to sit in the two front rows, which were roped off to segregate us from the white community. The government policies introduced in the 1960s were appalling. Adults were not allowed to be served in the local hotels, so they had to go around the side of the hotel where there were a couple of small windows, and the Aboriginal community was only allowed to buy alcohol from there to take away.

In 1965, I witnessed Charlie Perkins leading the Freedom Rides in Moree. This stirred up the Aboriginal community and many started up committees. When the 1967 Referendum was established, Moree set up an Aboriginal legal service, which my mother was actively involved in.

In 1969 a NAIDOC (formerly known as NADOC) committee was formed in Moree, and the first Miss NAIDOC contestant from Queensland came down to Moree for the NAIDOC week celebrations. My mum encouraged me to enter the Miss NAIDOC competition, a thought that was as obscure to me as flying to the moon. I had always considered myself as a bit of a tomboy. I used to go pig hunting with my brothers, and as it turned out, I was a pretty good shot, better even than my brothers. Reluctantly, I did enter the Miss NAIDOC competition – and to my surprise, I won.

This prestigious award provided many benefits, including trips to Sydney, Brisbane and the Gold Coast. The Lord Mayor

I was crowned Miss NAIDOC in 1969, with partner Danny Rose.

of Sydney presented me with a key to the city. There were many first-time experiences, including going to several populous cities, travelling on a plane, having media interviews and photo shoots. It was at this time that I met Darby McCarthy, a horseracing jockey who took a shine to me. We formed a close relationship and got married. We had our two sons, Jason and Bradley, while we lived in Brisbane and stayed there in 1971 for a couple of years. Then we moved down to Melbourne in 1973, where Darby continued his horseracing career. We established a new life together there, although we divorced in the late 1970s. I continued on as a single parent. Later on I had one more son, in 1981.

When I moved to Melbourne I met Harry Williams, a country music singer who played a regular gig in Fairfield with his band, the Country Outcasts. I learnt to play the bass guitar and eventually began to play country music in an all-Aboriginal female band called Ebon Koorines, which means Black daughters. We played at various venues around Melbourne from 1976 to 1980. We had a great time. There were four of us in the band – Roslyn Johnson on drums, Janice Johnson as lead guitarist, Debbie Williams on rhythm guitar, and I was on bass guitar. We all sang and harmonised.

Clockwise from top left: Me and the band; with Johnny Day; the Ebon Koorines: Roslyn on drums, Janis on lead guitar, Debbie on rhythm and me on bass guitar; the Mercury Blues: Richard Franklin and Grant Hansen, my brother-in-law.

In the mid 1980s Archie Roach began writing songs, and Janice, Roslyn and I joined him in a band. That is how Archie's career began. Eventually we ladies left because we had children at school and found it too hard to juggle time and travel commitments, indicative of life in a band. I did continue playing in other bands, however – such as the Koori Connection, Interaction, Stray Blacks and Mercury Blues – in the 1990s around Melbourne and rural Victoria. We played mainly rock n roll music from the

1950s and 1960s. I loved music and relished my involvement in these fun times. Music was always in my family life. My dad played guitar, and he taught me and my brothers, Garry, Ted and David, how to play when we were teenagers. My brothers played in bands in Moree on the mission. Back then it was a wonderful outlet for the community.

I commenced work in 1975 as an Aboriginal health aide, until my role changed to an Aboriginal Hospital Liaison Officer at Dandenong and St Vincent's Hospitals in the late 1970s. This included supporting families to safely navigate the hospital system. I was diligent in ensuring clients understood the importance of following patient care plans and medication usage. I stayed in this line of work until the mid 1990s.

Working as an Aboriginal liaison officer within the hospital system around Melbourne, I recognised a need for residential rehabilitation services for Aboriginal people. I was a founding member of Ngwala Willumbong, from its inception in the late 1970s right up until the early 1990s. I managed the Galiamble Men's Recovery Centre in St Kilda from 1998 to 1999 and then established the Winja Ulupna Women's Recovery Centre.

In the mid 1990s, I was elected onto the Aboriginal and Torres Strait Islander Commission (ATSIC) and served four years – first as a regional councillor and then two years as Victorian Commissioner – and was selected for a second term in 2000. During this time, I was instrumental in establishing recurrent funding for 3KND, an Indigenous radio station. Then I secured funding to establish Djirra, an Aboriginal-led organisation offering a suite of programs for the prevention of family violence, and legal services for Aboriginal women and youth.

In 2002, the organisation was officially established, and I have held the role of chairperson for over 15 years. The launch began the journey of developing and building the organisation, which continues to grow today.

During my term as Victorian Commissioner for ATSIC, I represented Victorian Aboriginal people at the United Nations in both New York (on numerous occasions) and Geneva, sitting across the table from government. The papers I presented were about health, substance abuse and human rights. As Commissioner, I worked at a state and national level as well as on an international platform. My role included being a signatory to the first Aboriginal Justice Agreement, signed off in the year 2000 – the only agreement of its kind in Australia. From this, a network of Aboriginal justice advisories was established and grew from five advisories to nine, across Victoria. This then formed an Aboriginal justice caucus that contributed advice to the government.

After my second term as Commissioner, I returned to Ngwala Willumbong Aboriginal Corporation as the Manager of

Me with former prime minister John Howard.

Residential Programs. Then I moved on to become a Project Officer on the Closing the Gap initiative with the Department of Health.

For over 40 years, I've dedicated my life to working and supporting the Victorian Aboriginal community – in the areas of health, justice, housing, drugs and alcohol, and family violence prevention, and as a conduit between state government, NGOs and ACCOs (Aboriginal Community Controlled Organisations). I am a solutions seeker and a strong advocate for Aboriginal and Torres Strait Islander youth. I like to be proactive in improving services for Aboriginal people and promoting self-determination. One of these actions was lobbying for Aboriginal gathering places to gain Neighbourhood House status, which attracts funding.

I ended my full-time career as an Aboriginal Health Project Officer, and retired from full-time work in 2016 to care for my son. However, I remain actively involved in the Aboriginal community through involvement on various committees and boards.

I have been a member of the Dandenong & Districts Aborigines Co-operative in Victoria for over 30 years, and in 2021 I was elected onto the board of directors. As well as being appointed to the Youth Parole Board in 2019, I am also the chairperson of the Southern Metropolitan Regional Aboriginal Justice Advisory Committee, which covers 10 local government areas.

I was a recipient of the Victorian Justice Award, and won a 3CR Community Award. In 2020 I won the Frankston/Mornington Peninsula NAIDOC Elders Award for leadership and advocacy work.

Aunty Helen Belle Bnads

Aunty Helen Belle Bnads

My father, Percy Bell, is from the Birri Gubba people and the Bindal group near Ayr. He was born on the Cherbourg Aboriginal Mission, located about two hours from Brisbane on the lands of the Waka Waka. It was a government-run mission from 1904 to 1986, with dormitories and a camp. Many of the men, young and old, were sent out to work as cheap labour for landowners in the surrounding area, and women were employed as domestic servants. An Aboriginal training farm at Cherbourg was established, where the boys were trained in all aspects of farm work. After learning these skills, they worked on the settlement or were sent away to work for pastoralists around Queensland. The government administration controlled what they ate, what they wore, where they went and the language they spoke. No one was allowed to practise Aboriginal culture or speak of it.

My paternal grandparents are also from Cherbourg and a lot of my cousins are buried there. Dad was from a large family and many of his siblings were born on Cherbourg Aboriginal

Mission. Some people gave up their Aboriginality and wore dog tags. This term was used when referring to certificates of exemption – licences that allowed an Aboriginal person to move freely about town, vote, drink at public bars and send their children to the local school. It was a way that the welfare board ensured that Aboriginal people assimilated into the white mans' world. In doing so, they were expected to renounce their culture, language and family ties. Others called themselves Māori, Spanish, Islanders – or anything to avoid stating that they were Aboriginal. My father was later taken from the mission and placed on a pastoral station.

My dad never spoke of this time in his life or the impacts it had on him and his family. When I went to university, I began to question him about what happened. We often walked and talked and one day I told him that all Aboriginal people have a file. I then said to him, "I'd like to see yours." He responded by telling me that I could see it when he had passed away. It left me with so many questions.

Dad was a man who worked very hard. He was taken from the mission at the age of 13 and placed on a pastoral station, where he learnt about horsemanship and farm work. He rode bulls and entered into rodeos, applying his riding skills to competition events. On the whole, my father was used as slave labour as a young man, due to the directive of the 'native affairs' government office. They were assigned to be in charge of the children of Aboriginal families. Many Aboriginal and Torres Strait Islander people were not paid for their work. It is often referred to as the Stolen Wages.

So, when Dad died, I wanted to know what had happened to him. I spoke to Mum about this and she agreed to sign the

My parents, Percy and Ivy Bell.

permission forms releasing his files to me. The information was staggering. He had written regular letters from the pastoral station where he worked, requesting boots to wear, a bar of soap and a swag to sleep on. These basic requests were not readily provided. In addition to this, the minimal money that he earned at the pastoral station was sent back to the mission. They let him have a bank account, although the mission only let him have a small amount of his wages. The mission kept the rest. Dad ran away from the pastoral station when he was 16 and met my mum not long afterwards. Mum was pregnant with their first-born child a year later. My dad never smoked cigarettes or drank alcohol. He died at age 60.

My mother, whose name was Ivy Monica Appoo, came from Apple Tree Creek, where my maternal grandparents lived, a rural town in the Bundaberg region of Queensland. Mum's lineage comes from Sri Lanka, although her mother was Irish. They all make up who I am today.

I was born in 1952, and I'm the second eldest of 10 children. One of our brothers died at birth. I grew up in Queensland and left my home in Brisbane, with full parental permission, when I was 15 years old. When our mob came to our house from the mission, mum would feed them. We had to sit on the floor while all the food was eaten in front of us. Finally, after several years, my parents bought our housing commission house and they lived there for 53 years. Mum stayed at home and cared for all nine of us kids, and Dad worked at various jobs. He always got work, even though he was unskilled. Their resilience inspired me and I drew from this through my own challenging times.

I had a thirst for knowledge, even though we never had pencils or books at home. My parents used to get up at 3am every morning to heat up the boiler to wash all our clothes. I would get up at 3.30am so that I could spend some time with them alone in front of the fire. I cherished those moments we had together.

I suffered terrible racism at the state primary school I went to in Brisbane. My destiny was impacted by ill health. As a child I contracted tuberculosis and I also had severe eczema. Because my family were financially poor, food was scarce. This meant that I never had the vitamins and minerals that my body craved. I always had bandages covering my sores, which were raw and very painful. I looked like a leper. Every night, Mum would soak my hands in Condy's Crystals so that she could peel the bandages off and treat the sores on my hands. These childhood experiences guided me to become a nurse. I understood what it was like to be sick all the time and to be in pain constantly. I identified a bigger purpose to my experiences of ill health – I learnt the importance of showing kindness and compassion, whatever a person's medical needs or the colour of their skin.

As a young child, it was challenging to have these problems – to experience racism as well made my early school years unbearable. Finally, I told my parents what was going on at school. I was seven years old. My parents were always busy looking after us 10 children and I had tried to avoid adding to their problems. My parents were shocked and went straight to my primary school to talk to the teachers and headmaster. The bullying came from the teachers – not allowing me to go to the bathroom, ridiculing me and humiliating me in front of a classroom full of kids.

I can recall when we used to write on chalkboards at school. One day we were learning mathematics and I wrote the answer on my board. The teacher accused me of cheating in front of the whole class and then sent me to the headmaster, who proceeded to hit me hard with his cane. This punishment was used on most of the kids but for me it was excruciating as he repeatedly whacked my hands, which were already bleeding and painful from the eczema.

I went home and told my parents, who acted on this immediately. After the bullying and racism from the teachers had been addressed and my parents ensured that their complaints were recorded, I left that school. My mother, a devout Roman Catholic, enrolled me into a Catholic primary school. I felt safe and supported there, and the nuns encouraged me to excel at my schoolwork. I enjoyed learning and craved intellectual stimulation. Entering this new school was life changing for me.

I used to look out of my bedroom window in our small three-bedroom home and yearn to get out. I knew I was loved. However, I felt a calling to experience life elsewhere. When I was

14 years old, the nuns (Daughters of Charity) told my parents that I'd make a good nurse. They wanted to take me down to Newcastle to begin nurse training, assuring my mother that they would look after me there. I jumped at the chance and left home after completing Year 10, aged 15. After my parents gave their permission, I caught the first train from Brisbane to Newcastle. My career as a nurse began at St Joseph's Nursing Home. I was the only Aboriginal person working there.

I felt very supported by the nuns during this time as I explored life through teenage eyes. The nuns had been encouraging me for years to join the convent. So one day, at the age of 16, I turned up at my parents' place and showed them the papers that the nuns had given to me to sign up to be a nun. Mum was happy for me to go – however, Dad was not. He picked up the papers and ripped them up. He looked at me and said, "You're not meant to do that!" Then he walked out without saying anything further. I was upset and confused. My father was a man of few words. I decided not to be a nun.

Later on, I left Newcastle to go back to nursing at the Mater Hospital in Brisbane. It was at this time that I met my husband, Bobby, at a nightclub. We were both 18 years old and fell in love straight away. He had come from Melbourne to compete in a wrestling competition, and he won an Australian wrestling title. We both felt we were destined to meet on the very night he was celebrating his hard-earned achievement. I came to Melbourne at age 19, got engaged at 20, and I married Bobby when I was 21. We have two daughters together.

This is when I decided that I wanted to go to university to further my education. I was about 32 years old when I studied, first law and the arts, then anthropology, human geography, archaeology and also history. I loved it and felt completely at home in the academic world. I was at Monash University for eight years.

My happiest memories are family orientated. I was part of a non-Indigenous family with my husband's relatives and I felt really supported and loved. We were all very close. In my late 30s I graduated, and my parents came down to Melbourne to celebrate my academic achievements. I am the only one in my family to leave Brisbane.

I have held roles in palliative care and counselling, using, among other things, narrative therapy – listening, observing, bringing compassion and empathy to clients. Some of my most significant work was being involved in the Link-Up Queensland initiative, where I worked closely with members of the Stolen Generations at graveside reunions. I felt privileged to be there when Aboriginal families saw each other for the first time since their forced removal. I also value the opportunity to work with those who are dying in

My daughters, Beth and Nadine.

palliative care. I like to be able to give them the caring attention they require and to see them off from this life with respect.

In 2019 I was selected for the Victorian Aboriginal Honour Roll. As I originally came from another state, Queensland, I was really moved that the Kooris here in Victoria nominated me, a Murri, for this prestigious award.

I am currently working on a reconciliation action plan for employment within Peninsula Health. It has taken two years to create new approaches to employing Aboriginal people within the Peninsula Health hospitals and community centres, and to ensure that people have pathways to further themselves through employment and education. After this has been completed, I will go back into palliative care.

Persistence despite our obstacles, along with underlying planning, results in the personal development of resilience – the ability to adapt to adversity and control individual responses. Resilient people find a solution and break the pattern of learned helplessness.

I have always wanted to be a positive example for my children and my grandkids. Life is short, and I believe we need to be the best we can in life. It starts by respecting ourselves first, and not giving up! Stay on your path and be consistent. Live life fully.

Aunty Karan Kent

Aunty Karan Kent

(Née Karan Williams)

My life began in 1959 at a little house adjoined to the main Box Hill Hospital. I was the third of five children and we grew up in Warrandyte, Victoria. Dad (Allan John Williams) was a boilermaker and Mum (Heather Jean Prince) was a stay-at-home mum from Augathella in south-west Queensland. Mum was taken from her family as a very small child, along with her five siblings. She remained separated from her parents until her early teens.

My grandmother, Nellie May McCann, was Irish and my grandfather, Philip Prince, was a proud Bidjara man who fought in WWI across England and Europe, including in the Battle of the Somme. When he returned home, he began rebuilding his life and had six children. By the early 1930s their children had been taken one by one, in the black police car. Mum, along with her two sisters, was put into Nazareth House, a Catholic orphanage for girls, where she stayed until she was 14 years old. The boy's were taken to St Vincent's Orphanage in Nudgee, a home for boys. According to the policies of the day, the children were

My great-grandmother Jane Boyd, 1930s.

removed because they were considered 'half-caste' and therefore better suited away from their Aboriginal parents. The aim of these policies was to assimilate them into a white Australia, and people were told that by doing so it was anticipated that Aboriginal culture would just die out.

When Mum was eight years old, she would be sent out each day to work for the local doctor's family, as a domestic in his home. She was expected to cook, clean and look after their three young children. Mum was never paid for her work. When she reached the tender age of 14, she was told she had to leave the orphanage. Her bags were packed and she was shown out the front door. Her elder sister, Ivy, was there to meet her.

Mum hadn't known that she had three brothers, as she was only a toddler when she had been taken from her family, and she was unsure who her two sisters were. Hearing about this as

My paternal grandmother, Nellie May McCann, 1920s.

My grandfather, Phillip Prince, WWI, 1916.

My mum at school.

a teenager from her sister, who was 10 years older, was a huge shock to her. None so big, however, as finding out that her mother had worked in the laundry at the orphanage the whole time she had lived there. My grandmother was told that the condition of her employment was that under no circumstance was she allowed to make contact with her three daughters while they were there – this included not talking to them or hugging them at any time. If she did, she would be dismissed instantly. Her job meant that she could lovingly watch over her daughters while they were at the orphanage, so she told no one who she was, so as not to jeopardise her position in the laundry. She stayed working there until all her daughters left the orphanage.

During this time, my grandfather had re-married and fathered a further six children, who all lived with him. When Mum found out about her family's circumstances, she was completely overwhelmed and struggled to comprehend it all, having been closeted in the orphanage for so many years.

A few years after finally leaving the girl's home, Mum went travelling. She visited Tasmania before making her way back to Melbourne, where she met my dad, an ex-WWII serviceman. Dad never spoke of the terrors of war and used alcohol as a way of dealing with post-traumatic stress disorder, a condition we didn't understand at the time. At home I remember the stark differences between my parents' beliefs – Mum was raised as a strict Catholic, and Dad was an atheist. Dad wouldn't let Mum practise her religion – so she had to sneak out of the house when he was boozed up on alcohol, so she could secretly attend church services.

No one at home talked about what had happened in the past, although we knew it was a time shrouded in fear. On rare occasions Mum would tell us about "the black car" that would "come

My mum.

get us if we didn't behave ourselves." As a child, I remember being scared of the black car. Mum had vivid memories of that fated day when she was taken from her family in a black car, and they haunted her throughout her life. I felt her fear when she spoke of it, a reminder of a dark past.

My parents bought a block of land in Warrandyte in the early 1950s. Dad was a proud man and planned to fulfill his dream of building a family home. The finishing touches, however, were never completed.

Our home, built on concrete stumps, consisted of four rooms – a bedroom, kitchenette, bathroom and main room. I slept in a big bed in one room with my two sisters. I was the youngest at the time, although Mum was pregnant with another child. The main room included our bedroom, as well as the dining and lounge area. Down the hallway there were a couple of floorboards missing and the cold wind always blew right through the house. The only television was in our parents' bedroom and was really high up on top of a large wardrobe. With only a cement sheet at the end of the hall, the house was always cold in the winter. My sisters and I would put our feet up on the wood-fired oven door in the kitchen to warm up.

As there was no running water connected to our old house, Mum would take my sisters and me for a 20-minute walk along a track to the Yarra River, to collect water in buckets. Once back home, we would fill a baby's bath that sat in the unconnected claw-legged bath, and all three kids would bathe, one at a time, using the same water.

Then one day the council sent us a notice informing us that our house was deemed uninhabitable, and that it would have

Mum with me and my three sisters, 1965.

to be demolished. With the prospect of a forced move, my parents decided to demolish the old place and build a brand new AVJennings home on site. We all got stuck into demolishing the old building, making way for our brand new home. We lived onsite in a caravan for some time while our new home was built.

From 1970–73 I attended high school. However, family life was challenging and I became a rebellious teenager. Dad had broken his back in a work accident and was made redundant. He never worked again, and drank more and more alcohol. Mum was pregnant again with her fifth child.

In the summer months I'd escape from home for some respite and catch up with my friends. I loved to explore our surrounding area. The bush, the river and a nearby tunnel became my favourite places, and I could always connect with the spirit people there. I struggled to focus on my schoolwork as I was restless and unhappy at home, so I left high school at 14 years old. Feeling ready for the 'real world', I got a job in the city. Keen to start straight away, I lied about my age. Each day I travelled 1.5 hours on a bus to get there, until my sister and I found our first flat to rent.

It was during these formative years in the early 1970s that I started to explore my Aboriginality. At home we had always been told that we were Māori, Indian or Southern Islanders, never Aboriginal. My uncles and aunties were darker skinned than I was, which always made me wonder why I was different. I can remember when they sat around a fire in our backyard singing haunting songs about the struggles of life. Every time I'd ask my parents about my Aboriginality, I was ignored or told not to ask any more. It was always an unspoken topic at home and our cultural connections were never acknowledged.

My curiosity to know more about my heritage continued, and I met up with some of the mob in St Kilda around this time, to see if I could find out some information. However, because no one knew which mob I belonged to, they didn't accept that I was Aboriginal. I felt rejected and knew that my paler skin and freckles added to people questioning my identity. Finding my Aboriginal family lines has been a lifetime quest.

At 15 years old, my sister and I moved into our first flat in Greville Street, Prahran, and we made new friendships and enjoyed many new social events. This is when I met a friend at work who introduced me to her brother, who turned out to be my future husband. We got married in 1978 and have remained happily married for over 45 years. By 1980, our eldest daughter was two and I was pregnant with our second child, so we began looking for a family home to buy. At this time, our combined income was about $50 per week and the average price in Parkdale, Victoria, where we lived, was around $25,000. In Cockatoo, however, we found one for $17,000. We settled into our new home, enjoying the natural habitat surrounding the area. The sound of the noisy cockatoos and the abundant bird life there was magnificent.

One day, in the heat of summer in Victoria, the kids and I were at home preparing for a special dinner that night. It was my husband's 33rd birthday, and we had made him a birthday cake

My husband and I on our wedding day.

with the candles on it, ready to light after dinner. We needed to get a couple of extra things before he came home from work, so I decided to walk through the bush that afternoon with my daughters, past Emerald Lake to the local shops. Being heavily pregnant, it was more of a slow stroll. I was nine months pregnant and due to give birth to our third child at any time.

During our walk it suddenly dawned on me that the bush had gone quiet. There were no screaming cockatoos, in fact I couldn't see any birds or wildlife at all. There was an eerie silence that actually scared me. Everything seemed strangely still, suspended in time; even the big gum trees surrounding us drooped in the heat. It was 16 February 1983 – Ash Wednesday.

We hadn't even begun dinner when out of nowhere our neighbour came running up the backyard, warning us that fires were coming. We thought the smell of smoke was coming from the Upper Beaconsfield fires, not Cockatoo. We acted immediately, trying to decide what to take as we prepared to leave the house. I noticed the little things – the dry washing folded neatly on a chair, the clothes for our unborn child stacked up in a corner ready for the birth, and hubby's present sitting on the kitchen bench. All of a sudden, we heard a helicopter hovering above our house and a voice booming through a loud speaker saying: "Evacuate, evacuate … evacuate NOW!"

My husband tried to hook up the boat to his car, while I put our daughters in the back of my old Hillman Hunter. As the smoke came closer, I panicked and reversed it into a tree, stalling the car. I could see the smoke with bursts of fire on top of the nearby hill, and it was heading straight for our place. Smoke billowed across the road too, and we couldn't see the gum trees surrounding us. There was a fire truck trying to fill up with water on the corner of our street, and one of the firemen, struggling to attach a fire hose, yelled across to us: "Get out of here now!"

My husband came over to my car and put our daughters and me into his car. I was panic stricken with fear. We heard gas bottles exploding and people screaming. Cars blocked the road as they all tried to escape. At some point we grabbed our dog, but she jumped out of the car and ran into the bush. There was no time to chase her, as we had to leave immediately. We could only pray for her safety. We escaped to a safe area at the top car park near our local shops, where we watched the flames lurching up in angry bursts and dancing on the horizon, making their way towards the township.

The following day, when the fire had subsided, we went back to assess the damage. Everything was scorched; the stench of burnt bush was overwhelming and the heat emanating from the ground was suffocating. The sky was on the ground. We were used to seeing the rich green gum trees that filled the entire space all the way to the sky. Astonished, I stood there barefoot. In my haste to get out of our house, I had left without wearing any shoes. The ground was so hot that it was unbearable to stand on, so I hopped around to avoid burning my feet. One of the SES workers gave me his size 10 thongs to wear, an act of kindness that I have never forgotten and still to this day brings happy tears.

We stood in shock at the devastation caused by this ferocious fire. Our house, the boat, our car and all our belongings were gone. From that point onwards our lives changed forever. All we had left was my husband's car and the clothes we were wearing on that fateful day.

Friends of ours offered us a caravan to stay in, and we used an outside toilet. Eventually we set up two sheds to make our temporary living quarters functional. Our makeshift home, which sat in an open paddock, was now visible to the public. Sightseers came in droves to view the destruction caused by the fires. Our street was now full of cars, whose drivers were continually stopping to have a look at the devastation caused by the fires. Our once secluded life was now completely gone. We had no privacy. Our life was exposed for all to see.

Two weeks later, on 5 March 1983, I gave birth to our baby boy. Living conditions were challenging, particularly with a newborn child and two small kids. Our eldest daughter had started kinder that year. For the remainder of her kinder year, she drew all her pictures in black and white, with no colour at all – the effects of the fires were shown in many ways, and for many years afterwards.

The generosity from the community was phenomenal. One woman, who we never knew, gave us a box of French vanilla cakes every week for months and months. We really appreciated these lovely gestures of kindness during those tough times. The strength and support within our community were extraordinary and the spirit of generosity unforgettable.

I remember some humbling moments when, because we didn't have any belongings, we had to rummage through the charity bins, better known as 'tent city', to find clothes for the kids and ourselves. There were many lessons we gained from surviving these horrific bush fires. I used to save our nice crockery for special occasions, or only use a little bit of my favourite perfume to save it for that special occasion, but when everything is gone, it changes the way you see life. Now I say: "Enjoy what you've got while you've got it – make every day a special day."

We all stayed in the two sheds for almost 10 months, while we rebuilt on site. As time went on, though, we found that the loss of some of our precious items became too upsetting. We struggled to settle in, as we were constantly looking for something that was gone. Our nerves were still on edge, raw from the impact of such a traumatic experience. We jumped at the sound of sirens or helicopters, and the smell of smoke made our fears resurface again and again. Because of this, we decided to start afresh, so we moved to Queensland.

I began researching my family history, so I pursued my investigations while living there. My cousin had also begun researching our family history and our combined information uncovered our lineage to Bidjara Country in south-western Queensland.

Over the past 30 years or so I have attended a number of family reunions and discussions with family members have confirmed where we are from, although there are a few who still believe we are connected to the Māoris. My journey of discovery has helped me gain a lot of clarity about my ancestors and strengthened my identity.

After living in Queensland for about five years, we moved back to Melbourne. Our eldest daughter became pregnant, so I became a grandmother at age 36. We now have 13 grandchildren, two grandchildren in heaven and four great grandchildren. We are a closely connected family and feel very blessed to be together.

After gaining a diploma in community development and then studying for a bachelor degree, I worked with Aboriginal communities in various roles for over 30 years. We moved to

Frankston in 1999 and met a local Elder within the Aboriginal community there. She embraced me as Aboriginal straight away, even before she heard Mum's story. Aunty and I formed a strong bond in those early years, and through that relationship I finally felt accepted within the Aboriginal community for the very first time. I finally found my home.

Aunty was one of a handful of local Elders who were involved with the foundational stages of establishing a gathering place for the local Aboriginal community of Frankston and surrounding areas – this led to the development of Nairm Marr Djambana gathering place, which I became involved in back in 2007. I remain a proud foundation member.

I can remember when the two buildings were placed at Nursery Avenue in Frankston, Victoria. One was for Nairm Marr Djambana and the other for Baluk Arts. Baluk Arts eventually moved to their current location in Bruce Street, Mornington and gifted their building to Nairm Marr Djambana.

My life has taken me on many journeys, with some twists and turns along the way. I'm honoured to have worked across local governments, Aboriginal health sectors and not-for-profits. Now, in my 60s, I'm a sole trader and business owner.

I'm most proud of my cultural commitment to community, and have had the privilege of being involved with Local Aboriginal Educational Consultative Groups (LAECGs) and Koori Engagement Support Officers (KESOs) providing advice to schools through Cultural Understanding and Safety Training (CUST). In addition to this, I currently hold the position of chairperson for Dhelk Dja, in the south metro region of Victoria and am a respected Elder within the Koori Court.

My journey through life has empowered me with a strong connection to my Aboriginal identity. I value my birthright and culture. I would love to see Aboriginal culture taught in schools and integrated as part of our national curriculum, so that future generations can learn about the oldest living culture in the world and be proud of our heritage.

Uncle Graeme Donald Beamish

Uncle Graeme Donald Beamish
(Beamo)

I was born during WWII, on July 1941, at the Royal Women's Hospital in Parkville, Melbourne. My mother, Victoria Boddington, was also born there. She is a Yamatji woman from Western Australia, although she grew up in Carlton, Melbourne. I was taken from my mother when I was three months old and placed into an orphanage. Then, one day, Mrs Myrtle Beamish and her husband Wally came to the orphanage and chose to adopt me, along with my sister, Berris, who they had adopted previously. Myrtle and Wally had three daughters of their own, Joan, Margaret and Laurel.

I didn't go to kindergarten. However, when I was four years old, I was told I would be staying with my Uncle Fred and Aunty Dorry at their orchard property in Shepparton, northern Victoria. No one explained why. I stayed there for six months. Fortunately, I enjoyed being with my uncle and aunty, although it was a mystery to me why I was there.

Then, back in Melbourne, when I was old enough, I went to school. We lived at Park Crescent, in the Melbourne suburb

Jack Bonsak and Victoria (Peggie) Boddington.

Jack and Peggie on their wedding day.

of Boronia. I hadn't long been at school when I was taken away again, this time to the suburb of Blackburn. It was the middle of WWII and I recall seeing a guy who lived in the neighbourhood driving an army tank around the streets. He told me he wanted to convert it into a bulldozer.

I found out many years later that my mother, Victoria Boddington, had been looking for me. She wanted to see how I was doing and to re-connect.

However, Myrtle and Wally made sure that this never happened, by moving all over the country to avoid her. I recall that day vividly, when one of my elder sisters told me the truth. She thought it best that I knew, as I was being teased by some of the kids at school, saying: "Your mother's not your real mother." I went home one day and confronted Myrtle about these rumours. She kept saying, "I'm your mother", and refused to talk about it any further. I was nine years old.

My childhood years were very confusing, as I was shuttled from one place to another, with no explanation given to me by my parents. When I reached my teens, Myrtle placed me into Winnington Grammar School in Ringwood, that is until I was taken away for a final time to an area called Casino, in New South Wales, where I stayed in a small town called Tabulam. I went to school there, and my sisters Joan and Margaret worked in the medical team with the Australian Red Cross.

We moved back to Melbourne again, to Park Crescent in Boronia, where I finished my high school education at a state school, although I struggled to catch up with the other students, due to all the moves and changes that occurred during those formative years. I lost interest in schoolwork and

Peggie and my sister, Liz.

My brother, Gary.

my grades dropped. I felt a strange sense of displacement both at school and at home. Myrtle wouldn't allow me to pursue alternative learning through TAFE, so I went out to work. I was 14 years old.

Myrtle wanted me to be a ticket writer and took me into Myer store in Melbourne to get a job there. My wage was just over one pound a week. I attended Melbourne Technical College in the evenings to learn how to do the lettering, but after six months I left. I was focused on earning more money, so I found another job, one involving silkscreen printing. This time my wage was 20 pounds a week, which meant I could save up for my own car. Twelve weeks later, I bought my first car for 40 pounds. I was thrilled to bits. It was an iridescent blue 1941 two-door V8 Ford. I drove it home to show my parents, but Wally told me not to park it at our home. He was completely unaware of how much it meant to me. I was 17 years of age and still had to wait until I was 18 to get my driver licence.

Once I could legally drive, I looked further afield for work and landed a job in a wrecking yard, where I earned 30 pounds a week. Most people my age were out working at this time. One night I was with a mate of mine, and through his connections I met my future wife, Trish. I was 22 and Trish was 15. We moved into a house at Ferntree Gully, before I asked Trish's father if I could marry her. He gave his consent and we got married the following weekend.

We moved back to Park Crescent, Boronia for a while, when Trish became pregnant. I came home from work one day just as an ambulance drove out of our street with its siren blasting loudly. It was Trish being rushed to hospital.

She gave birth to our son, who we named Shane. We left my family home and moved into a small one-bedroom flat. We were young parents, Trish was 17 and I was 23 years old. Shortly after, I left to get some work up in the Snowy Mountains, so that we could set ourselves up in a more stable environment.

Trish stayed with our friends while I was away, and I drove up north with some mates who were also seeking work. After a long trip, we checked into the work site but unfortunately discovered that the company had offered all the jobs to the Greek and Italian immigrants. So, we drove into Sydney and I got a job as a bricklayer's labourer. A few weeks later I went back to Melbourne to see Trish.

When I arrived, Trish told me that the Department of Human Services (DHS) had taken our son away. Myrtle and one of my sisters had visited Trish and decided to bring someone from DHS around to remove Shane from our home. Shocked and distraught, I rang the child welfare department straight away to find out why they had taken him from us. They told me that we needed to prove to them that we could get a house of our own.

We moved to a place in Dandenong called the Spud House. It consisted of lots of little rooms with a bed in each one and a shared bathroom. There was a dining room upstairs where you could get a reasonable meal – a large potato, vegies and meat – all for 10 dollars a week. It was a way that we could get ahead financially, so Trish and I both worked hard and saved our money.

Then, one evening after work, a lady came to visit us. She was from the DHS and wanted to check on us to see how we were progressing, or at least that's what we thought. We showed her how much we were saving. However, she took us outside and told us to get in to the back seat of her Austin A40 car, which was parked by the building. It was dark outside and the little light shining in the car was dimly lit, making it hard to see clearly. The lady from child welfare handed us some documents and told us to sign them, right there and then. We asked what the papers were for, and she assured us that it was so that they could look after Shane until we had enough money to get our own house. She didn't explain anything to us, or say what we were agreeing to.

They took our son off us and placed him into another home, somewhere in Melbourne. We had trusted her and were blind-sided by a decision that regrettably changed our lives, and our son's. It was a shock and deeply affected us. We had little choice but to make a fresh start, so we moved to Emerald and I worked on the Thomson Dam project, where I earned $150 per week. Trish worked at a local drycleaner's. By now I was about 30 years old and Trish was in her 20s.

I was drinking heavily and smoking a lot, and Trish helped me to see this. I made my mind up to give them both up one night, and I have never smoked cigarettes or drunk alcohol since. Trish burnt her hand while working at the drycleaners and she was paid two thousand dollars' compensation. We used this money to buy a caravan and we moved to Frankston.

While living there, we were involved in a car accident, which caused some serious injuries to Trish. The police confirmed that the other driver caused the accident and suggested we get some legal advice. We were told that we could sue for damages. Trish had a brain injury and a broken neck, which was not detected straight away. Eventually, Trish received a payout and we decided to use that money to buy our first house in Frankston.

After many years experience as a bricklayer, I realised I had the basis to establish my own business. I worked at it and eventually had 78 contractors working for me. Once I had secured a successful business, I built our own home in Frankston and I'm still living in that house today.

During this time, Trish decided to do some extensive research into finding our son. We found him and he was living in Melbourne. He was in his early 20s. After speaking with various people, we were told that we could see him. We were beyond excited about this, after all this time. A couple of days later, we received a call to say that Shane had been hit by a car and died immediately. We were devastated.

A few years later, we decided to move to Queensland, and lived there for about eight years. We loved it there and relished the opportunity to enjoy some time together. After some challenging times and a lot of hard work, we were finally able to enjoy the fruits of our labour. Unfortunately Trish fell ill, so we moved back to Melbourne. She went into hospital six times in a row for more and more tests as her health deteriorated, until she was finally diagnosed with cancer. She passed away shortly after. I miss her every day.

I would like to see more young people learn about their rights, so they can make informed decisions and find out their true identity.

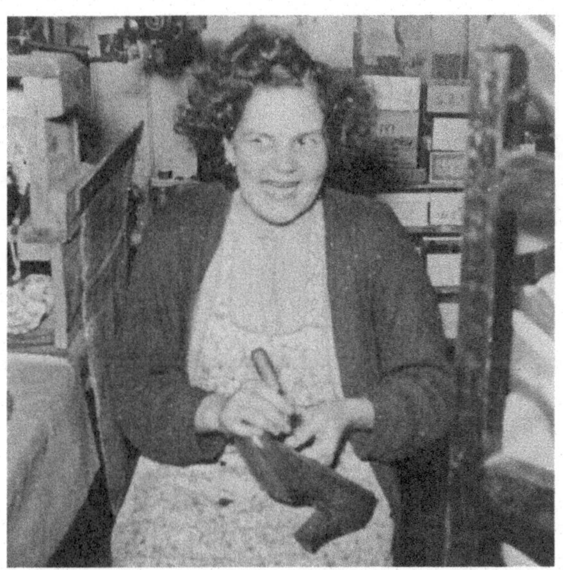

My mum Peggie Bodington at Goodchild Shoe Factory in Croydon.

Me and Trish.

Aunty Diane Aiello

Aunty Diane Aiello

I was born in 1959 at Diamond Valley in Greensborough, Victoria. My Aboriginal lineage links to Western Australia with the Willum Yamatji mob. My earliest memories are when we lived in a tin shed at Panton Hill, a town in Victoria, 32km north-east of Melbourne's central business district. We lived in the middle of nowhere. My older brother and I used to walk for miles up the long dirt road to go to school. I was five years old and remember the school tuck shop, because there was nowhere else to go to in the area. My older brother and two younger brothers and I used to just hang out together a lot. We had an old hermit who stayed on the property where we lived, in a little tin shed. He just needed somewhere to live. He would collect beer bottles and sell them, as a way to survive. He helped us by cleaning up around the outside of our house.

We lived in a two-bedroom shed with an outside toilet out the back. Us four kids all slept in one double bed and we bathed in tin tubs. There was a creek nearby which provided food for us to catch, and we cooked on a very old oven. Our main food source was chicken. Mum used to hatch them and when they were older, my brother would cut off their heads and I would have to dip them into boiling water and pluck them. Mum would make a bit of money from the chickens.

One day I fell out of a tree and when I landed on the ground, a stump went into my back. Mum had to gather us all and take us to our neighbour, who lived about an hour away, to get me to hospital. Fortunately, there was no lasting damage caused by the fall. Dad had left us some years earlier, until one day he turned up. He told us that he'd found another girlfriend, and she'd given birth to their baby boy. She ran away directly afterwards, leaving her baby behind. So, Dad asked my mother if she would raise him. Mum already had four children she was raising on her own, so she said no. Dad left again, and as it turned out, he ended up raising him himself.

My mother, Emma Dixie, is one of 10 children, and is from Western Australia. She was forcibly removed from her parents and brothers and sisters, and then placed into Sister Kate's Children's Cottage Home, an orphanage in Geraldton, until she was 18 years old. Her brothers were placed in another orphanage for boys.

In the early 1900s, the Western Australian legislation allowed appalling intervention into the lives of Aboriginal families, some of the most extreme in the country. Under the Aborigines Act 1905 (WA), Mr Neville was the legal guardian of every Aboriginal child. By 1915, he had become the Chief Protector of Aborigines.

Sister Kate's Children's Cottage Home was established in Queen's Park by mid 1934, when Sister Kate Clutterbuck, an Anglican nun, pioneered a cottage home system for looking after

Mum (at the back) with her sisters Kathleen, Annie, Hilda and Vivian Dickerson.

orphan babies and children. She was well known for her care of young children and ran the home for nearly 30 years, caring for over 800 children. The home was funded by the Aborigines Department to house 'fair skinned' Aboriginal children. After Sister Kate's death in 1946, the home was taken over by the Uniting Church and conditions began to deteriorate.

Not long after Mum was released from the orphanage, she met my dad. Mum worked up around the Kimberley doing fencing, jillaroo work and gold mining, and she also worked as a cook at cattle stations. Because Dad was in the airforce, he wanted to move closer to his family in Victoria, so they moved to Melbourne. Dad and his sister owned quite a lot of land there, although his sister decided to sell it, and that's why we had to move back to Panton Hill.

This time, I was about seven years old.

The house was right up high on top of a steep hill, and when we went to school each day we had to walk down the hill, along a windy track and over a creek. We had to edge ourselves across a log that lay over the creek, a challenge every day but more so after torrential rains, when the water level rose right up to the log, gushing furiously beneath us. We held on tight to a long piece of wire that stretched over the water. Mum would always stay on the opposite side and guide us. She trusted us to get over it, and we did.

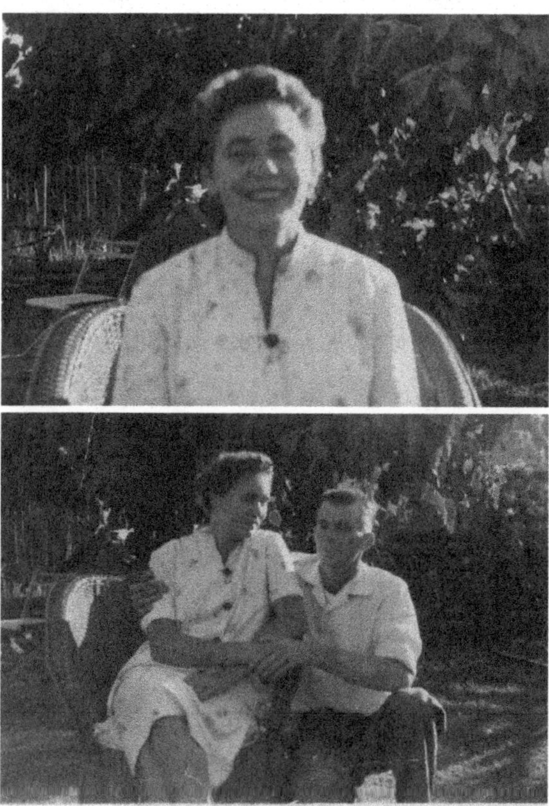

Top: My mum, Emma McCudden.
Bottom: My mum with her first husband, Brian McCudden.

Then we had to walk across two paddocks, and the horses would see us and come running over, looking for food. It was scary seeing them galloping towards us. Finally, we had to walk across a main road to get to our school. This was our daily routine, every week, to school and back.

The two-bedroom wooden house we stayed in had big windows at the front and an outhouse at the back. We four kids all shared a double bed. We lived there for about a year, until a tragic incident happened that changed all of our lives overnight.

It was nighttime and we were all at home. Then suddenly Mum grabbed me and told me not to make a sound. She took me outside, and we hid in the bushes. Mum looked at me and said, "Don't move!" There were two local policemen standing at our front door, shouting, "If you don't come out, we'll kill your sons," who were sound asleep in their beds. We came out of hiding and they raped my mother. I can remember this all very clearly – I was so frightened. It was traumatic. The threat they made to kill my brothers forced my mum to put us into Allambie Reception Centre, a children's home in Burwood, Victoria. I was eight years old. She saved my brothers' lives. My mum then moved to the city.

Allambie Reception Centre accommodated girls (2–14 years) and boys (2–10 years), and had the capacity for up to 90 children in four separate sections. During the 1960s and 1970s there was a significant shortage of suitable options for children and young people, and many stayed at Allambie and Turana for very long periods, worsening overcrowding.

Mum came to visit us nearly every day at the orphanage. I learnt to swim while I was there, although six months later I ended up with hepatitis, which I had contracted from the orphanage. They took me to Fairfield Hospital, where I stayed for three months – literally fighting for my life. My skin colour turned yellow and my liver and kidneys were shutting down. I couldn't see anyone during this time. I felt as if I were in a glass cage, in a room with windows surrounding me.

Then we were transferred to the Children's Home in Box Hill, Victoria. I found out later that this was an Aboriginal orphanage – although the children staying there did have parents. There were about 20 to 30 kids there at the time, and they had all been taken forcibly from their parents. Mum visited us every weekend and bought lollies for everyone, which we shared out so that all the kids got something.

The staff at Allambie didn't get my mother's permission to move us into the Children's Home – in fact, they didn't even notify her. Because of this, it took Mum a few weeks to find out where we were.

During the time Mum was looking for us, my younger brother was almost adopted out to an American couple. Again, our mother was not notified that such an arrangement was being made – without her permission. I can remember how angry my mum was about this.

Not long after this Mum met Dad, and she bought him down to the orphanage to see us. He asked her, "Are these all my children?" Right then Mum knew he was the right one for her. They got married and stayed together for the rest of their lives. His mother was strict and conservative and her old-school English ways stayed with her throughout her life. Dad lived with his mother until he was 40 years old. Even after he married my mother, he used to visit her every day before he came home to us.

Mum marrying my stepdad, Ronald Cooper.

She sternly told my mum that Dad wouldn't be paying for her or her kids. I was just rapt to have a grandmother.

We lived in Seaford, where my dad bought a house and both my parents worked. Mum worked at Bata shoes for many years, and then she worked nights cleaning houses in Mt Martha and Mt Eliza. I supported Mum by helping with the chores at home and looking after my brothers. From the age of nine I had to cook, clean, get my brothers ready for school and then walk them there. Then, I'd go home and get dinner ready. I'd go babysitting at night, and that money would go straight to Mum to pay for food and bills. This was my routine every day. By the time I went to high school, I had a younger sister and so I had another lunch to make in the mornings before I would walk all my siblings to school.

In the weekends we'd work at a commercial baiting business, where we would shell pipis and put them into bags. We'd work for a whole day, either on a Saturday or a Sunday, and we gave that money to Mum too. If I wanted to earn some extra money, I'd ask people at a local retirement village if they needed some weeding done. The times we kids relished was when we could go bush. It felt so good to be among nature.

In the 1960s and 1970s, occasionally Dad would go down to the pub with his mates. Sometimes Mum would have to ask us kids to go and get him and bring him home. Mum's pleasure was putting the odd bet on the horses at the TAB. She would spend a whole Sunday studying the horses and then ask us kids to walk down to the betting shop to put a 20-cent bet on a horse for her. I don't remember her ever winning anything.

My friends were my brother's mates. I was used to my boisterous brothers and I found them easier to be around. The girls at school were often catty. Our food at home was made into meals that fed all seven of us. We ate ox tongue, brains, tripe and everything from inside a cow or a sheep. We had a lot of stews, often made up of three chops and vegetables. It was first in, to get one of those chops.

One old house we stayed at, near Safeway in Seaford, was haunted. We never went upstairs. All five of us kids slept in a big

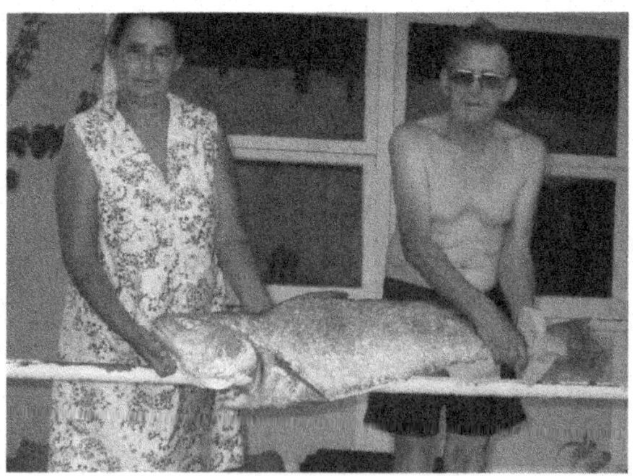

Aunty Annie and dad, Ronald Cooper.

double bed together downstairs. We used to fish for eels in the creek nearby, and we'd go digging for bardis (witchetty grubs) for Mum. She loved them.

Dad would do anything for us. He loved us all. Sometimes I'd find some coins on the floor in my parents' room, and I'd feel pretty chuffed having some spending money at school. Later on, I found out that he'd left the coins there deliberately for me to have.

Mum always wanted to go back home to Western Australia. We took a trip there once in our old station wagon. There were four kids and three adults squeezed into our car, including Nana. We travelled from Seaford to Geraldton, in Western Australia. It took us a while, but we got there eventually. Mum was so thrilled to finally see her brothers, sisters and cousins. It was a very emotional reunion for them all.

Geraldton was a very racist town, particularly from the 1970s to the 1990s. Mum and Dad went to the pub when we got there. There was a pub for Blacks and a pub for whites. So, Dad went to the Black's pub with Mum. When we left, Mum wanted to bring my uncle back with us, as he had diabetes and needed some care. Unfortunately, there wasn't enough room in the car for my uncle to come back to Victoria with us, as I had invited a friend of mine to join us on the trip. I was about 14 years old then, and I didn't quite think as an adult, although this was often expected of me as the eldest child. My uncle was blind, and tragically he got hit by a car and died some years later.

Ironically, I first met my husband when I was about 12 years old, when one day he came over to our place to sell a motorbike to my brother. I remember thinking back then that I was going to marry him, and I did. We met again when I was 16 and we went out together. Later we got married, and have been together for 44 years. We've had four children together. My husband's Italian family welcomed me into their family from the start. We moved to Somerville on the Mornington Peninsula, and got a housing commission house as our first home.

My mum lived to 59 years old. She worked hard all her life, although for many years she was unwell. She was diagnosed with cancer and was given six months to live. When Mum's family found out over in Western Australia, they sent us a medicinal plant in the form of sticks. The Elders would dance and then do a ceremony over them before they sent them to Mum. When they arrived at our place, only Mum was allowed in the room when she opened the parcel. Then Dad would boil them up and mum drank the liquid every day. This enabled her to live a further three years.

As a mother myself, I remember panicking when I had my first daughter. I thought the government might take her away. Even when I had my second daughter, I still feared this could happen. My mum was forcibly removed from her family, and so was I. Generational trauma is very real.

I did a lot of cultural awareness programs with kids at kindergartens and at schools, through stories, artwork and role-play. I would love to see this introduced into school curriculums. I am a passionate artist and have sold a lot of my own artwork overseas – in Germany, America, China, Japan and Italy. I won the 2006 NAIDOC Artist of the Year Award.

I have been proactive in establishing the Aboriginal gathering place in Frankston. Through negotiations with the Frankston City Council and the Department of Human Services, we finally established Nairm Marr Djambana. This has been operating now

Mum with Aunty Hilda and Uncle Sammy.

for over 12 years. In addition to this, I helped set up the first NAIDOC Gala Ball on the Mornington Peninsula in the year 2000 with Shyvonne, one of my daughters. Throughout my life I have drawn from Mum's courage and determination. Nothing would stand in her way, and she inspired me to achieve outcomes I didn't think I could achieve. Never deny who you are. Be strong and be proud of your Aboriginality. We are, after all, the longest living culture in the world.

Aunty Dawn Campbell

Aunty Dawn Campbell

(Née Dawn Cook)

I was born in Tasmania in October 1955 in a little country town called Leslie Vale. I am the fourth of 12 children. We lived in a little tin hut, so we enjoyed simple pleasures. There were seven siblings in the family back then, and all of us kids curled up together, keeping each other warm in the big double bed, which was in our parents' room. The table and chairs were near the fireplace in the lounge room. We all had to help out with the daily chores – gathering firewood, setting the table and boiling water for washing up after meals.

I was born deaf and dumb. When my Aunty Daphne and Uncle Jack used to visit us, they taught me how to read and write and helped me to talk clearly. Aunty Daphne was such a wonderful support and encouraged me to learn. She paid for numerous operations that I had over the years, on my voice box and on my ears. One day, Aunty Daphne and Uncle Jack approached my dad and asked him if they could adopt me. They wanted to help me in the best possible way, so that I could have a good education.

Unfortunately, my mum said no.

Once I learnt to talk, my parents wanted to send me to a special school. However, I wanted to go to a normal state school. The other kids teased me a lot there, but I found my strength and soon learnt how to stand up for myself. It shaped me into who I am today.

My Aboriginal grandmother, Dorothy Forster, was stolen from the riverbanks in Tasmania when she was young. For many years she worked out in the fields, until one day when she got a job as lady-in-waiting for a woman who had arrived from England. My nan lived with her in her home, along with an English gentleman by the name of Alexander Forster. He fell in love with my grandmother and they got married. Known among his close family, friends and colleagues as Alex, he was respected in the community. They had a daughter, my mother, Phoebe Eileen Forster. Mum was one of nine children.

When I was a child, I recall a time when I went to the see the doctor with my nan. They were talking and she said, "You know I'm a Black person?" He responded immediately, "There's no such thing as the Black fellas here, and you're not! Keep quiet!" As a young girl I felt confused by the doctor's indignation. I didn't understand why he spoke to my nan like that.

My dad, Royston John Cook, was a builder working with a team of men, building houses in and around Hobart. When I was in Grade Four, we moved into a house in Davey Street in Hobart. It was a big house and I remember walking up the path towards the front door and seeing all the colourful flowers planted in two rows in the front garden. Each row had flowers of the same colour and were planted from the smallest plants to the largest, near our front door. One day two policemen knocked at our front door. My mother was shocked when they told her that there were some opium poppies growing among the mixture of plants.

We had fruit trees at the back of our house, a variety of berry plants and plenty of space to run around. When I was about seven years old, I remember the fun my brothers and sisters and I had, including times when we used to climb down the drainpipe and sneak outside to play, without our parents knowing. We had an electric stove and a wood stove. We always used the wood-fired oven and we'd all huddle around it to keep warm. My dad fought in WWII, risking his life every day as he searched for land mines. He was hit one day by an exploding mine and a piece of the shrapnel embedded itself into his head. The doctor decided, after examining it, that it was too dangerous to remove, so it remained in the side of his head. He met my mum when he got back after the war.

My youngest brother, Mum, my nephew, me and my youngest sister.

When I was about 14 years old, I went to a school swimming carnival and lost my voice. I couldn't talk at all. My parents took me to get examined and were told that I needed another operation on my voice box. After this, my parents separated. My mother asked my father to leave, so he moved into a boarding house nearby. He came to see us kids every Thursday evening after work, and he would bring us some ice cream. A week after I had the operation on my voice box I was able to speak again, and the first words I uttered brought tears to my father's eyes. My caring father gave us all sixpence that day, which was a lot of money back then.

Then, one evening, he didn't turn up. We waited and waited for him, sitting patiently until midnight. The next morning, we

My dad, Royston John Cook.

My daughter Chantelle, my son, Simon and me.

Billy and I getting married.

My late husband Billy and my mum.

heard an announcement on the radio, stating that someone had been bashed and run over in Hobart. My second eldest brother wondered if it was our father and went to the police station to inquire. The policeman described the tattoo that my father had on his arm, so he knew it was him. As the story unfolded, it looked suspiciously like foul play. My father had been involved in a poker game the night before, with some of the men on the building site he was working on, and he had won a lot of money. He left work and was on his way to the bank to deposit his winnings when he was attacked and killed. His wallet was gone. I was very close to my dad.

I left Tasmania in my early 20s, and moved to Victoria. I got married to Phillip in 1983, and we had three children together. Things didn't work out for us, so I moved down to the Mornington Peninsula with the kids. I linked up with the Aboriginal community and began teaching Indigenous culture to some of the young children, with Anglicare. Then I met Billy and got married at Dromana in 2007. Over the years I fostered some children too. Later on, I worked alongside the local police, assisting young Aboriginal people while they attended court proceedings.

I would like to see more support for young Aboriginal people – building their confidence and self-esteem as they grow and develop.

Aunty Roseina Woods

Aunty Roseina Woods

(Née Roseina Nona)

I was born on Thursday Island in 1953 and I'm the eldest of 12 children. I grew up with my family on Badu Island in the western side of the Torres Strait islands. My Aboriginal mother and Torres Strait Islander father raised us in the traditional Island ways – we spoke broken English, ate turtle and dugong and grew sweet potatoes and pumpkin in our garden. We didn't have gas or electricity in our home, which meant we had to walk for many miles every day to collect water and firewood to cook food for the whole family. Being the eldest daughter, I would often end up with this task. I used to carry the water on my back. The water was needed for cooking and also for washing, so it was important to make sure supplies were replenished each day.

A staple part of our diet was fish, and living in the Torres Strait Islands surrounded by the ocean meant there was an abundance of seafood. However, the area around Badu Island was tidal and fishing trips required some effort, paddling a dinghy for miles from the shores to reach deeper waters, where there were more fish.

My father was the Chief of the Islands and often hunted turtle, dugong and wild pig to provide for all the families living on Badu Island. Dugong was cooked similar to meat, in stews or fried. His regular job involved being in the water every day from 6am to 6pm, as a pearl diver. He would deep-sea dive looking for pearl shells, which were plentiful in the northern waters.

Damper, scones and rice were also eaten regularly and everyone helped with the daily chores. I started working at 18 years old at the hospital on Thursday Island as a nurse earning $30 a week, which went towards the upkeep of the family. Back then the focus was on getting a job, not a career. The Torres Strait Islands are made up of 32 small islands. Horn Island is where the planes came in, and Thursday Island is the main island with the only

My father, Nona Nona.

hospital and port. We used the CB (citizens band) radios for communication across the islands, a job I often was asked to do.

I went to boarding school at the Atherton Tablelands in Queensland and nurse training college in Cairns. When I went back to Thursday Island I was promoted to the role of Head Nurse at the hospital. I found it quite different from the isolated life on Badu Island. In Cairns there were white kids and mixed cultures together, whereas white people were not permitted to come to the Torres Strait Islands. Islanders were told that this was to protect their communities from influences such as drugs or the spread of diseases. Papua New Guineans were not allowed to visit either, even though towns such as Daru traded bananas and clothes with Badu.

My mother, also a nurse before she had children, came from a large family of 10 children, and my maternal grandmother was stolen from her family in the Weipa district of the northern Queensland region. She was one of many Aboriginal women taken by immigrant sealers who came to the shores along the tropical coasts of the Gulf of Carpentaria.

On Badu Island there was one state primary school, which we all attended. When I was about 12 years old Queensland Premier Sir Joh Bjelke-Petersen visited the Torres Strait Islands and came to Badu Island. I was chosen to present him with a trophy, in appreciation of his coming to the Islands. In the normal way, the children would often sit under a tree to learn English, and for this special occasion my teacher helped me to prepare a speech and practise pronouncing my words in English. It was a celebrated event and my mother made me a special dress with a big bow at the back of it. I even had to curtsey to the Premier.

My father, Nona Nona and my mother, Gikana Nona.

The family home on Badu Island was built out of slate and got very hot during the summer season. There were no bedrooms in the house. The front verandah acted as a bedroom, although all 12 of us children lined up on the concrete floor and slept in the main room on big Island-made mats. My father bought a wire-woven bed and when he went away, the kids and I would fight over who should sleep on it.

Responsibilities came with being the eldest child, including many tasks at home. On weekdays, I had to get up at 6am every morning to help my mother prepare breakfast for my siblings, and on the weekends I had to rake the yard and do the washing for the family. It took an hour to walk to our local school, and at the end of a school day we often felt tired after the long walk back home again.

One day, after much thought, I decided that I wanted to leave the Islands, asserting my rights as a young adult. I had met a contractor at the hospital while I was working there. He was building houses on many of the islands. I asked him to stow me away secretly on his boat to Thursday Island. Even though he was a little fearful of getting caught he agreed, and I packed a bag and hid in the speedboat as they travelled from Badu back to Thursday Island.

My exit was not without its challenges, as the government policies stated that a permit was required to leave the islands. This meant that I had to go to the court on Thursday Island to explain to government officials, my grandfather Tanu Nona, and my parents, why I wanted to leave.

Although my parents supported my decision to go 'mainstream', as they called it, 'down south' to Cairns, I still had to face my grandfather. Fear of breaking the law among the Islanders was common and in addition to this, my family was held in high esteem.

In 1972, my grandfather's brother, a pearler and politician of Sāmoan and Torres Strait Islander ancestry, received the prestigious OBE medal for his dedicated contribution to the Island communities. Operating pearling boats along the coast of Queensland from the 1920s until his death in 1980, he enabled businesses to flourish by providing Islanders with ongoing work opportunities. In 1959 the Nona family controlled eight vessels and accounted for well over 50% of the catches of the government fleet.

The Nonas and their associates also provided skippers for four boats in the industry's private sector. Badu Island prospered greatly throughout this period and the feasts were among the most opulent in the Torres Strait.

So, for me to leave the Islands was not as easy as simply saying goodbye. My grandfather, Tanu Nona, told me to go back to Badu, but I had made up my mind and insisted that they allow me to leave. After some forthright discussions at the courthouse, I was given a permit to leave the Islands.

During this time, I had been selected by the hospital on Thursday Island to go to the nurse training college on the Atherton Tablelands to do some further nursing training. However, I chose a different direction.

I had my sights set on working in hospitality, where a weekly wage was much higher than what I had received while working on the Islands. Moving down south, I stayed with my aunt and got

Uncle Tupoa and Aunty Enaine Nona.

some work in Weipa, a coastal township on the west coast of the Cape York Peninsula.

A mining region rich in bauxite, it attracted contract miners, and this work was a main source of income there. I worked for several years in large canteens, cooking meals, waitressing and running the facilities for the men working there. I enjoyed the work and travelled to Kakadu and Brisbane for similar roles.

When I took some time off to visit my family back at Badu, many of my extended family called me a 'southerner' because I had left the Islands and chosen to live in Queensland. Eventually I got married and moved to Melbourne, where we had two children together. I have lived on the Mornington Peninsula for about 30 years, and have worked with local councils, raising the Torres Strait Island flag and giving speeches to the community during NAIDOC Week in Frankston, Rosebud and Dandenong.

My fondest memories are of my childhood growing up on the Torres Strait Islands with my family, and even though life was tough at times, I believe to this day that young people should work to get ahead in life.

Uncle Steve Delaney

Uncle Steve Delaney

I was born in 1954 at Katoomba (Dharuk Country) in New South Wales. However, I believe it is my father's side, the Kamilaroi mob, that influences my lineage the most. My father, William (John) Delaney, was stolen from his parents twice – once when he was only six months old and then again when he was about three. My brother asked my Nana Delaney what the story was behind my father being taken. Nana eventually told him what happened, but asked him to promise never to ask her again. The trauma connected to the memory was too painful for her to talk about. I am one of six boys and one stepsister in my family, although our youngest sibling died just after his birth. For many years, when I was young, we lived at Woy Woy, a coastal town in the Central Coast region of New South Wales.

My Nana Delaney was forcibly taken also – from New South Wales to Horsham, then to Lake Tyers and from there back to New South Wales. Later, she took her 14 children and walked hundreds of miles to protect her kids from being taken from her. They finally settled in Taree, at Rainbow Flat. She was an incredibly strong woman.

Because we were disconnected from our past, we never learnt about our culture or family history. Even when my father got older, he would only share stories and cultural knowledge with my children, but not me. When the movie *Rabbit-Proof Fence* came out in 2002, I watched it, and it moved me. The prayer that they said before they ate was the same prayer that Dad taught us. It broke me up.

We moved around a lot. When I was about 14, we went up to Queensland to live. It was very racial there and I copped it pretty hard because I wasn't as dark as others were within the local Aboriginal community. My skin tanned a dark brown in the summer months, but I was never really accepted as an Aboriginal.

At that time in my life, my parents only touched on the fact that our father was in an orphanage, so I struggled to understand who we were or where we were all connected to. Dad was the eldest boy of 17 children, and the eldest three were forcibly removed.

My parents settled down at Eastern Creek, New South Wales in the late 1960s and lived on the Great Western Highway, a major thoroughfare. They always had their Aboriginal flags and banners up. Then we started travelling around. I found out later on that the reason for this was because Dad was trying to find his family. During this time, my grandmother and aunties had also tried to find my father. This happened twice, although we didn't actually meet them.

We were staying in Redfern with some relatives, while my father worked in Sydney. I was about four years old and playing with my Dinky Toys when my natural grandmother, Nana Delaney, and

Dad's sister arrived at the front door. I told my parents and relatives that there was someone outside, then all of a sudden all of us kids were shuffled out to the back of the house, and the relatives who lived in the house sent Nana Delaney and my aunt away.

They were left crying at the front door. My father never knew who they were, as he was only a little boy when he was taken. He eventually met up with his mother when he was in his mid 60s, and they finally spent some time together.

The family we stayed with treated us harshly. At Christmas time, because they had a large family, we were expected to wait until everyone had eaten their meal, before we could start ours. There was about 20 of them sitting around the dining table. When they had finished, we had to clear the table, scrape all the leftover food into one or two plates, and that was our Christmas dinner.

In my early 20s, I went to Groote Eylandt, an island in the Gulf of Carpentaria, to work. I was a boilermaker and had completed my four-year apprenticeship. I met an Aboriginal Elder while I was there who recognised me, and my connection to the Kamilaroi mob. He looked at me and said, "You and I are of the same blood." It meant so much to me to know this. Later on, my uncle (my dad's younger brother) and I rode our motorbikes for many miles, visiting people in Queensland, New South Wales and in Victoria, to learn about our family history and who we are connected to.

In my late 30s, I had a major accident doing maintenance work. This caused me some serious physical damage, which prevented me from doing the trade work that I had trained in for many years. This forced me to change my line of work and to explore different opportunities. Later on, I did blacksmithing and then moved onto automotive structural engineering. I received recognition from the Rolls-Royce headquarters in England for the engine work on boats I had done during this time.

I took the road of academic learning and gained three qualifications – an Advanced Diploma of Community Development, an Advanced Diploma of Legal Practice and an Advanced Diploma of Indigenous Studies. Working in the area of law in both New South Wales and Victoria for many years, I became the first local Aboriginal justice worker in Victoria, and initiated the Closing the Gap program. I was on the board as well as being involved in the program.

Prior to this, I was a sessional supervisor for the Department of Justice in New South Wales. This entailed bringing young, at-risk Aboriginal people into a program that I developed, called Guraki Thrawa. This was designed to prepare marginalised people for employment, and was delivered through the TAFE institute at Taree, in New South Wales. I had spent some time gaining support from local people and businesses beforehand. Then, because of the success of this program, I was asked to be a relief Juvenile Justice Officer for the Department of Justice in New South Wales. I did this for about seven years, working within the community, attending stakeholder meetings and attending court proceedings. This work led to a further role within the justice system, as an Aboriginal Justice Worker in Kempsey. I was given over 500 cases to work on, an overwhelming number – however, I slowly worked through them all. At one point I had 28 court reports on one day. I continued this job for almost nine years. I discovered at this time that I was a diabetic and this forced me to make a lifestyle change.

I returned to Melbourne in 2006, after 12 years of travelling and living in various places around Australia. With many years of experience behind me working within the judicial system, I was asked to work directly within Melbourne prisons – Marngoneet Correctional Centre, the Metropolitan Remand Centre and the Melbourne Assessment Prison. I facilitated programs for men on mental and physical health and relationships. I did this for about eight years. Earning respect was key to maintaining close relationships in that role.

I was also asked to attend the County Court as a respected Elder. I sat at the table to provide the judge with insights into cultural understanding for Aboriginal cases, and to give an analysis of recommended preventative measures tailored to each case. I talked to the perpetrator directly, raising their awareness and accountability for their actions.

In addition to this, I helped develop and co-facilitate the longest running Aboriginal men's group in Victoria, called Tjeagen's Warriors, named after a valued young member of the community. I found that during the many years I worked with young people, I observed that all of them had been victims of abuse. Young people are fragile. I experienced abuse myself and understand first-hand how this can affect a person during those formative years and the transition into adulthood. I felt lost and angry.

Not having the right sort of care and guidance during this crucial transition in your life can be detrimental. This is what motivated me to get involved in the judicial system. My work with youth involved assisting them with ideas and approaches that guided them to make good choices in their lives, and to learn from their experience of being locked up. I used to tell them that although they had reasons for their circumstances, that is not an excuse for bad behaviour.

I would sometimes share my personal experiences of my traumatic childhood and youth with my young charges, so that they could hear other people's situations, to understand that they weren't alone. For example, the day I was to start primary school I endured my first horrific experience. I was five years old, and my brother hung me up on a tin fence with a piece of tin stuck through my thumb. No one heard me screaming, so I hung there for some time in excruciating pain. I lost a lot of blood and required some time to heal.

My mother's form of punishment was beating me. She also used to insist that I get down on the floor and clean obsessively. For her everything had to be perfect, a form of psychological abuse that caused me to feel humiliated. Because of this, I rebelled throughout my youth. However, I learnt from my mistakes. Later in my adult life, my mum realised that I wasn't the person I had been when I was a young confused teenager. I couldn't give her a hug because she had belted this act of love out of me. Ironically, my mother had experienced the same treatment herself when she was young.

I have lived on the Mornington Peninsula in Victoria for many years and have been a founding board member for two Aboriginal organisations. In 2009, I was nominated as an emerging leader. I would like to see young people encouraged to learn in ways that inspire all students. After many years working with our young people, I would also like to see our society, and indeed our justice system, have a better understanding of the needs of youth today. I have taught Aboriginal cultural immersion programs for many years at various schools across the metropolitan area of Melbourne, and have seen the value that this brings. I would dearly love to see Aboriginal culture shared across society. Education is the key to understanding. My father wasn't allowed to share this. However, I believe it is incredibly valuable to all of us.